THE CONTRIBUTION OF INDIAN MUSIC TO MUSIC THERAPY

By
Vidhi Sharma

ACKNOWLEDGEMENT

First of all I express my heartiest and deep gratitude towards my supervisor, mentor and guide Late Professor Nupur Roy Chowdhury, Faculty of Music & Fine Arts, Delhi University, for her erudite and scholarly guidance given to me for this research work. It was her support that I could work on this knowledgeable and interesting topic for research, and got exposed to the dimensions of the wide scope of study in it. She has not only given me her priceless guidance and help in all study related matters, but also provided me with the support and encouragement in every matter of consequence to me. Her words have been a great source of inspiration for me, which have helped me to forge ahead every time with a renewed energy. I am deeply indebted to her. Now, when she is not there in this physical world, then also she will be present with me for lifetime. Her motherly concern will always be remembered.

I wish to record my sincere thanks and gratitude to Prof. Uma Garg, Head and Dean, Department of music, university of Delhi, for her gracious help on various matters form time to time. Through her kind support only, I have been able to submit this Research work.

I wish to record my sincere thanks and gratitude to Prof (Mrs.) Anupam Mahajan (former head and dean), Department of Music, University of Delhi, for approving my topic for research and also encouraging from time to time with her kind words.

I would also like to thank, Pt. Shashank Katti (Sitar Maestro and Music Therapist) and Sh. Murad Ali (Sarangi Maestro) for the time and knowledge they have provided for my research work.

I would also like to give my heartiest thanks to "The Library Staff", Faculty of Music and Fine Arts, University of Delhi for letting me use their precious books, "The Archeological survey of India" for helping me and providing the necessary information about my research.

I wish to express my heartiest gratitude to my first mentors in life, my Parents, Sh. Gurbachan Singh Sharma and Smt. Prem Sharma, who always inspired me to give my best to every task which I take on to. This research work would never have been completed without their constant motivation and blessings.

In the end I express my special gratitude to my entire family and friends who always blessed me and provided me with all the facilities essential for my research work and encouraged me at the toughest times. Without their support and understanding, this research work would have not been completed.

Vidhi Sharma

CONTENTS

Titles	Page No.
Acknowledgement	I
Introduction	1-6
Chapter 1: The Indian Music	7-54

❖ The significant origin and development of Indian Music.

❖ What comprises Indian Music

Chapter 2: Indian music as "The Therapeutic Healer"   *55-83*

❖ Nada Yoga.

❖ Nadopasna

❖ Chanting and toning.

❖ Raga Chikitsa.

❖ Tala, Rhythm and the Heartbeats.

❖ The primacy of the voice and the association of the musical sound with prayer.

❖ The healing power of *'AUM'*

Chapter 3: Music Therapy   *84-106*

❖ What is Music Therapy?

❖ The constitution of Music Therapy - Beyond the Boundaries.

❖ Role of Music Therapy in healing the Mankind.

Chapter 4: The contribution of Indian Music to Music Therapy   *107-149*

❖ The power of Sound.

❖ Self realization – the 'Goal of Hinduism'.

❖ Role of different forms of Indian Music in 'HEALING PROCESS'.

❖ The Power of "AUM"- Vibration defining the entire COSMOS.

Chapter 5: Formal & Informal Research done in the field of Music Therapy (In India and Abroad).   *150-190*

❖ Music Therapy in India.

❖ Music Therapy Round the Globe.

Titles	Page No.

Chapter 6: The Cultural Uniqueness and Togetherness of Music   *191-203*
          Therapy: A mix of Eastern and a Western Voice.

Conclusion   *204-208*

Abstract

The ancient system of 'Nada Yoga', which dates back to the time of Tantras, has fully acknowledged the impact of music on body and mind and put into practice the vibrations emanating from sounds to uplift one's level of consciousness. It is the Indian genius that recognized that ragas are not just mere commodities of entertainment but the vibration in their resonance could synchronize with one's moods and health. By stimulating the moods and controlling the brain wave patterns, Ragas could work as a complimentary medicine. This research work is an effort for the global acknowledgment to the role of Indian Music to Music Therapy, as well as for the welfare of mankind and wisdom of all disciples of music. The reservoir of this knowledge will prove a great help in increasing awareness on musical therapy. As, the Physiological, psychological, moral, intellectual and spiritual effects of music confirm the vital role of Indian music. All the forms of Indian Music which are related to different emotions in their own structures, compositions, rhythm patterns and the frequencies have their vital role to play in Music therapy like in ragadari sangeet the raga Miya Ki Malhar is for the monsoon season, when the great clouds are just about to burst, it begins with the tense note and ends in a crescendo of sounds. Thus, if played near a person emotionally charged up, it will help that person release pent-up energies and negative emotions. For instance,in semi classical musical forms such as thumri, tappa depict the explicit beauty of the emotions. Similarly folk music charges the cells with a lot of energy.

INTRODUCTION

INTRODUCTION

If we take a quick look into the historical background of music therapy, it was enriched, well formed and firmed in our very own country as a whole such as Nada Yoga, Nadopasna, Raaga Chikitsa, Chanting of Sama Veda, Toning, the primacy of the voice and the association of the musical sound with prayer were thus established and the most important aspect of the sound "Aum" which is considered the manifested sound or syllable which define the entire cosmos itself. Even Mantras have a scientific logic related to our seven chakras, as by practicing each Mantra we automatically heal our body.

Long before acoustics came to be understood in Europe as a subject of study, the ancient Indian civilization was already familiar with the therapeutic role of sounds and vibrations and the later concepts pertaining to them. While music as a whole is well recognized for its entertainment value, the Indian civilization had gone a step forward to attribute the curative aspect of music.

The ancient system of 'Nada Yoga', which dates back to the time of Tantras, has fully acknowledged the impact of music on body and mind and put into practice the vibrations emanating from sounds to uplift one's level of consciousness. It is the Indian genius that recognized that ragas are not just mere commodities of entertainment but the vibration in their resonance could synchronize with one's moods and health. By stimulating the moods and controlling the brain wave patterns, Ragas could work as a complimentary medicine.

Raga Chikitsa' was an ancient manuscript, which dealt with the therapeutic effects of raga. The library at Thanjavur is reported to contain such a treasure on ragas that spells out the application and use of various ragas in fighting common ailments. According to an ancient Indian text, Swara Sastra, the seventy-two melakarta ragas (parent ragas) control the 72 important nerves in the body. It is believed that if one sings with due devotion, adhering to the raga lakshana (norms) and sruti shuddhi, (pitch purity) the raga could affect the particular nerve in the body in a favourable manner. Some ragas like Darbari Kanhada, Kamaj and Pooriya are found to help in defusing mental tension, particularly in the case of hysterics. For those who suffer from hypertension, ragas such as Ahirbhairav, Pooriya and Todi are prescribed. To control anger and bring down the violence within, Carnatic ragas like Punnagavarali, Sahana etc. do come handy.

Legend has it that Saint Thyagaraja brought a dead person back to life with his Bilahari composition Naa Jiva Dhaara. Muthuswamy Dikshitar's Navagrihakriti is believed to cure stomach ache. Shyamashastry's composition Duru Sugu uses music to pray for good health. Here for the reference we can take the instance of music maestro Tansen, who by singing Raag Deepak was just about to burn his body and then came his daughter Saraswati, who sang the raag Malhar to decrease the heat in his father's body and saved his life. Ahh ! Immense power, Music has.

Despite of having this great and rich heritage which is like unexplored and uncovered treasure, the modern revival of Indian musical therapy is not yet sufficiently progressed to indicate its full utility in universal music therapy which is to be well identified by us Indians. It is obvious that the psychological effect of therapeutic music would be greater if the patient understood that the scientific foundation of the procedure had been thoroughly established.

This research work is an effort for the global acknowledgment to the role of Indian Music to Music Therapy, as well as for the welfare of mankind and wisdom of all disciples of music. The reservoir of this knowledge will prove a great help in increasing awareness on musical therapy. As, the Physiological, psychological, moral, intellectual and spiritual effects of music confirm the vital role of Indian music.

The music of India includes multiple varieties of folk, popular, pop, classical music. India's classical music tradition, including Carnatic and Hindustani music, has a history spanning millennia and, developed over several eras, it remains fundamental to the lives of Indians today as sources of religious inspiration, cultural expression and pure entertainment. The two main traditions of classical music which have been Carnatic music, found predominantly in the peninsular regions and Hindustani music, found in the northern and central parts. While both traditions claim Vedic origin, history indicates that the two traditions diverged from a common musical root since 13th century. Hindustani music is an Indian classical music tradition that go back to Vedic times. The practice of singing based on notes was popular even from the Vedic times where the hymns in Sama Veda, a sacred text, was sung as Samagana and not chanted. Developing a strong and diverse tradition over several centuries, it has contemporary traditions established in India. Besides pure classical, there are also many semi-classical forms.

The present form of Carnatic music is based on historical developments that can be traced to the 15th - 16th centuries AD and thereafter. From the ancient Sanskrit works available, and the several epigraphically inscriptional evidences, the history of classical musical traditions can be traced back to about 2500 years. Carnatic music is completely melodic, with improvised variations. The main emphasis is on vocal music; most compositions are written to be sung, and even when played on instruments, they are meant to be performed in a singing style (known as gāyaki).

The folk includes Bauls of Bengals, Bhagra of Punjab, Bhaavgeete of south, dandiya of Gujrat, Lavni of Maharashtra, Rudali of Rajasthan. Qawwali has the essence of Sufi, the unforgettable RabindraSangeet and diverse Rajasthani music.

All the forms of Indian Music which are related to different emotions in their own structures, compositions, rhythm patterns and the frequencies have their vital role to play in Music therapy like in ragadari sangeet the raga Miya Ki Malhar is for the monsoon season, when the great clouds are just about to burst, it begins with the tense note and ends in a crescendo of sounds. Thus, if played near a person emotionally charged up, it will help that person release pent-up energies and negative emotions. For instance, in semi classical musical forms such as thumri, tappa depict the explicit beauty of the emotions. Similarly folk music charges the cells with a lot of energy.

"MUSIC THERAPY" is a wider concept and has a broader perspective beyond the geographical, cultural, religious or any lateral boundaries. It knows only one object and that we can identify the healing of mankind. It comprises of all the vocal & instrumental, new age & classical music. The ancient musicologist and mystics of India and worldwide, who developed sound, observed that sound has an invincible power and the sound which is called "Nada" in Indian classic music is the base of the pyramid of music as a whole.

The scientific definition of Music therapy is based on the associative and cognitive powers of the mind. Sound creates certain vibrations which are picked up and amplified by the human ear. These waves are then being picked by the sensory nerves going into the middle of the brain and redistributed throughout the neural network to other parts of the brain to distinguish the pitch, tone and frequency of the sound.

Music Therapy deals with the cure of a many disorders. It utilizes music and music related activities to modify ineffective learning patterns, help to promote emotional, mental, social and physical growth and to develop non-musical goals. Music Therapy works as a creative, flexible and sometimes spontaneous means of utilizing the appeal of music to help people of all ages and abilities. Music Therapy is an established health care profession that uses music and "techniques" in order to address Psychiatry, Social Skills, Emotions, Communication, Self-Esteem, Relaxation, Cognition patterns. Music Therapy can positively affect children and adults alike. Music Therapy can make the difference between isolation and interaction and has been proven in situations such as depression, anger, pain, autism, stress, grief, loss, time management, motivation, growth, change, procrastination and improving communication.

On the basis of the above usage of musical sound, it is crystal clear that the music therapy which is based on the sound and rhythm is not the subject of an article only. The entire subject is now in the experimental and implementation stage and data are rapidly accumulating. And the ancient system is gradually being transformed into the modern science. A lot of research is happening on global panel. This Research work is an attempt to the extensive research on the Role of Indian music in music therapy, so that, the students of Indian music should also know about the healing role of Indian Music.

CHAPTER – 1

The Indian Music

- *The significant origin and development of Indian Music.*
- *What comprises Indian Music*

CHAPTER 1
THE INDIAN MUSIC

In reference to the topic, before discussing the origin and development of Indian music, it is necessarily important to pay attention to the very basic two grounds of the mankind's civilization, which are: Feelings and Intellect. Because, when we are supposed to have a look on the history then while doing so, we need to look for the ground or base first. Music, which is said to be the most powerful of all arts, has got a very solid base too, and that unshaken base comprises two strong pillars called emotions and mental ability. And, when these two pillars stand parallel to one another, they stand like the great building which usually represents the **society**. In a way society is defined as:-

> 'The more cultivated portion of any community in its social relations and influences; those who mutually give- receive formal entertainments'.

Relations are connected to feelings and emotions & influences have connections with intellectual and mental ability. On the basis of the association in between these two fundamentals, we can have a well-grounded thought formed and that particular thought exists in the name of society.

The history of music is closely associated with human society, so, it does not ignore the imaginative and creative faculty of man. It has rather a deep regard for the human society. Therefore, the sociological factors which are behind the creation of music can neither be neglected nor ignored, as it is really a product of the intelligence and creativity of the human society. In this context, Theodore M. Finney is of opinion that:

'Music emerged into the historic era as a social art and consequently its history can't be written without mentioning its social uses. The types of music may vary immensely, but the forms of its use, the purposes, for which any culture retains music as a part of its social heritage, remain almost the same.'

In truth, music is closely connected with human life from the very beginning of creation. Every nation or society made music their means to progress and prosperity, in social, political, cultural, religious and spiritual spheres of life. In the remote days all rites and ceremonies were connected with the elements of music. Our judgment on the worth of Indian music is based on the ancient music, works and traditions and here comes the **Society** with the use of word **Traditions**. Now, it will not be an exaggeration if it is said that art is the mirror of the social surroundings and followed traditions. And when it is about the great art Music, then we can look deep down into the history of Indian music to prove this point adequately. The history of Indian music should, therefore, be an authentic record of development of music of the Indian people.

The origin and development of Indian Music

The origin and development of Indian Music is hidden under the cover of developing Indian civilization. And in the history of India, we find that the civilized merchants really built the grand structure of culture and civilization of the prehistoric Indus valley of the remote past. Some hold that these builders were the Aryans, nay the Vedic Aryans themselves, who were the original dwellers of India and never came from Central Asia or from any other parts outside India. Others are of opinion that the original builders of pre-historic Indus civilization were the Dravidians and not the Vedic Aryans. These opinions related to the builders may differ, but we get ample evidences of the practice of music and dance, as obtaining in the pre-historic Indus Valley Civilization. The archaeological excavations of different ancient sites in India, which are considered by experts to be continuation of the Indus civilization and culture, disclose the fact that even in that remote age of 5,000 or 4,000-2,500 B.C., the people were most civilized, artistic and cultured, and they were well-conversant with the art of playing flute and lutes (vamsi and vina) and different types of drums (mridanga). But unfortunately we do not know the technique of their music and dancing, in the absence of definite system of notation and historical records.[1]

Indian music has extended itself from the antique pre-historic age to the present time. Actually it changed and evolved as inevitable for the shifting phases of changing circumstances of the human society. The gradual evolutionary process of Indian music is really a key to the whole range of musical production that flowed from the imaginative conception of the Indian people. Many old treatises and stone carvings are extant to record and commemorate the great art of India in different patterns, presentations and appreciations in different ages. Now, a question arises in mind, what is the utility of the study of the development of music and what is the importance of maintaining a historical outlook in the practical field of music. So, it is really required to answer this question before discussing the origin and development of Indian music, from the point of having a clear idea about the relation of Music with Mankind as a beautiful gift of god.

As we all know that factually man has an aspiring and progressive soul, and he always marches towards the ultimate goal of success, keeping his eye fixed on the golden ideals. On this point, Prof. Ogden is of opinion that:

'In the history of art as much as in any other branch of research, facts are meaningless until interpreted, and the function of the musical historian is, or should be, as different from that of the period-specialist as the function of the philosopher is from that of the chemists, physicists, biologists, anthropologists and other scientists who provide him with his material. His concern, in short, is not with the discovery of facts, but with their interpretation, and the revelation of their intrinsic value and significance.'

Pre Vedic Period

The oldest history of India is that of the Indus civilization. Mohenjo-Daro and Harappa are the two places where historical finds of Indus civilization have been discovered by the archaeological department. Harappa is at a distance of 100 miles to the south-west of Lahore, and Mohenjo-Daro is at a distance of 200 miles from Karachi. Terracotta seals, vessels, images of animals, statues, remnants of cities and forts go to prove that this was the most ancient civilization of India. It is considered to be at least 5000 years old. Some regard this civilization as pre-Vedic and some as Vedic.[1]

Among other finds were a flute, a harp with strings, and percussion instruments have also been found. A bronze figurine of a dancing girl beating time to music with her foot has also been found. This shows that people in that remote age knew the use of harp, flute, percussion instruments and the art of dancing. On the basis of this short data, we cannot say what the music of those times was like. We have, however, a more detailed account of the music of the Vedic times. Though, the diggings of the mounds of the pre-historic Indus Valley cities have astounded the people of the world, by furnishing some crude types of pipe, flute (veena) and drum of different sizes, together with the bronze figurine of a nude dancing girl, which prove the practice of music in the society at least five thousand years ago.[2]

The Vedic Period

The date of the oldest text i.e. Rig-Veda is variously estimated by scholars from 2000B.C. to 10,000 B.C.[1]The Vedas were musically recited in this musically significant period. The Vedic Music, Samagana was the earliest scientific method of singing in India. It became systematic when three base tones like anudatta, svarita and udatta evolved.[2] Udatta (raised), Anudatta (not raised) and Svarita (circumflex) were the three pitches used in Vedic recitative. Udatta was an acute or sharp pitch, Anudatta was a grave pitch and Svarita was a pitch which combined in itself the characteristics of both i.e., it started with Udatta and fell down to Anudatta. In Vedic literature, Svarita is called Pravana i.e., it gradually descended from Udatta to Anudatta. It formed a link between Udatta and Anudatta. These three were not merely accents or stress on the words; they were musical pitches used for simple recitation.

In the Rig-Vedic age (3000-2500 B.C.) we come across the proofs of political, social and religious organizations among the Aryan people. Their vast literature, undoubtedly prove that they were the most advanced people of that particular era. They use to perform sacrifices and sacred rites, and used to sing songs with different tones on many occasions. The rules and regulations, governing the songs, are found in the Siksas, Pratisakhyas and the Brahamana literature, and they also contain copious references of music of the Vedic time.[3]

Different kinds of lute (veena) and drum have also been described in the Vedic literature. The veena with hundred strings (vana) and kasyapi or kacchapi, picchola, ksauni, etc. and primitive drums like the bhumi-

---

dundubhi, dundubhi, etc. were used by the Vedic singers. The references are also found about dances, songs and musical instruments in the later Sutra literature. In the classical and the post-classical periods, many new types of veena like daravi, gatra, citra, vipanci, raudri, brahmi, katyayani, etc. and drums like puskara, bhanda, panava, mridanga, etc. also evolved.

While commenting on the Grihya Sutra, Dr. Apte has made references about music that was cultured by the Vedic people. He has said:

> "Music or sangeeta of all three types ('nrityam, gitam, and Vaditram') as well as chariot rares and gambling continued to be the principal amusements of this (Sutra) period. In the Samaveda (I.22.II) and the Asvalayana-Grhyasutra (I.14), we find descriptions of lute playing, dancing and singing, in connection with the simantonnayana ceremony. It is, therefore, proved that the Vedic people did systematically culture the art of music. The later Hindu society of India borrowed music from the pre-Vedic and Vedic people thus leaving behind a tradition of culture that enriched the art of music of India."[1]

Now it may be taken for granted that Vedic music was much more developed and systematic with its fixed tones and scales, and that the pre-Vedic and Vedic music owed much to the undeveloped system of music of the most ancient primitive people. The Vedic literature also furnishes various references of Vedic music. By 'Vedic music' we mean the samans with tunes. When the rik stanzas were set to tones and tunes, they were called the Vedic samagana. The samans used to be sung in different forms in different Vedic shakhas. The Pushpa Sutra and the Naradiya shiksha have fully described about those samans and different methods of singing.

The Vedic tones were used in the Vedic songs, and they were prathama, dvitiya, tritiya, chaturtha, mandra (panchama), atisvarya (shashtha) and

---

krushta (saptama). The tones of the Vedic music were in downward movement (avarohana-krama).[1]

Generally three, four, five and six tones were used in the samagana, and seven tones were used by the followers of the Kauthuma recension.

The samans, as mentioned in the Vedas and the Vedic literature, were the songs, set to tunes. According to Jaimani, the songs were but the internal efforts (abhyantara-prayatna) of the priestly class:

Sayana, the commentator, has said that the samas were the songs, constituted out of the rik stanzas and the tones like krusta, prathama, etc.:

> "Sama-sabdavacyasya gan asya svarupamrgakaresu krustadibhih saptabhihsvaraih aksaravikaradibhyasca nispadyate| krustahprathamodvitiyastritiycaturthah pancamah santhascetyete saptasvarah"| te cavyantarabhedairvabudha bhinnah."

It is said that the samans used to be sung with different modes and ways:

> "vahubhih prakarairganatmakamyat samasvarupam nirupitam."

Sayana has also said:

> "samavede sabasram gityupayah."

The samans were sung according to aksara-vikara (alteration of letters) like vislesana, vikarsana, abhyasa and virama. The stobhas used to play an important part in the singing.

Jaimani has said in the Mimansa-darasana (1.2.26):

> "sa niyatapramana rei giyate, tat-sampadanartho ya mrgaksara-vikaro visleso vikarasanamabhyaso viramah stobha ityevama-dayah sarve samavede samanayante."

The elongated letters like A......E......I......O......U, were known as stobha. In the present-day system of classical music, the stobhas are used with elongation of the vowels, which create vital force in the songs. To cite an example, the part of the songs: 'devadeva mahadeva gauripati mahesvara," etc. when sung as "de-eva-a de-eva-a maha-a-de-eva-a" etc. the elongated vowels are the stobhas. Regarding the stobha, Sayana has said:

"abhikatve satyrg-vilaksana-varnah stobhah"

The stobha was divided into varnastobha, padastobha and vakyastobha. Like the processes of mutilation and elongation of the letters in the stanzas, the method of obliteration or deletion of letters (varnalopa or aksaralopa) in the songs was also found necessary, and so Sayana has said:

"aksarvikara-stobhadivat varnalopoapi kacid gitiheturbhavati."

As for example, the words "agnaayahi" were uttered in the singing as "ognayi". This rule used to be specially observed in the geyagana, veyagana or vegana, yonigana, etc. In fact, the samans were composed and practised in different manners.

In the Rik-pratisakhya, the Vedic tones are called the 'yama'. The root meaning of which is 'to control' or 'to regulate'. So, as the tones use to control, conduct and sustain the structure of the samagana, they are known as 'yama'. The word 'yama' has been used in the Yogasutra of Patanjali to connote the idea of control: "yama-niyamasana-pranayama," etc. in truth the seven tones are the fountain head of not only of the scales and modes of the saman singing, but also of the later evolved raga, tana, murchana, alamkara, mela or melakarta, sthaya, prabandha, etc. and so they are regarded as the basis or ground of music of all times.

Some are of opinion that the tones of the Indian music are borrowed from the foreign nations like Arabs, etc., observing the similarity of names of the tones of both the systems, Indian and Arabian. But that is not the fact. The names of the Arabic tones are: jek, du, si, tschar, peni, schesch and heft (=sapta), and they resemble the names of the vedic tones, prathama, dvitiya, tritiya, caturtha, pancama, sastha and saptama.

The songs of Rig-Veda were known as giti, gatha and gayatra. Gathas were songs sung on the occasions of ceremonies and festivals. A song consisted of three parts and was known as stoma. The word sama has also been used in the Rig-Veda for song.[1]Various musical instruments were in use in the Vedic times. Among stringed instruments we find the mention of vana in Rig-Veda. In the whole Rig-Veda, vina has nowhere been mentioned. We find instead a mention of vana which was a bow shaped harp, with sometimes a hundred strings according to Sayana, the commentator of the Vedas. Vina has been referred to in Yajur-Veda which was composed later than the Rig-Veda, but vina was also at first bow-shaped. Among the percussion instruments, the one most frequently cited in the Vedas is the Dundubhi. Now a days it is generally called Naqqara or Nagara in Northern India. There were in the Dundubhi two drums- one big and the other one small. It was made by hollowing out a block of wood, and stretching an ox's hide over the mouth. It was played with a stick. It used to be played mostly in war, in the Vedic times. Later on, it was played also in the king's court, and in temples. Vanaspati was a wooden drum. Another drum that is usually referred to is Adambara. Gargara was another drum used in war. It is an onomatopoeic word. It used to produce the sound of 'gargar'. Aghati was a cymbal used for indicating rhythm. In the

Atharva-Veda, it is also called Aghata. Bhumi-dundubhi is another drum that one comes across in the Vedas.

Among wind instruments, we find a mention of Nadi and Nalika. Probably, bakura was also a wind instrument. Tunava and Sankha (conch) were other wind instruments. Venu or bamboo flute also came into use.[1]

In the Yajurveda, we find a reference to regular professional players of instruments who had specialized in playing particular instruments, for instance, Vina players, Tunava players, Conch-blowers, Aghati players, and Kahala players. Tunava was a wind instrument and kahala was something like the modern Shahanai.[2]

The hymns on Sama-Veda were sung in the well-defined tunes and according to the set rules. Sama-Veda is divided into two portions-archika and gana. Archika contains only the texts of the songs while the gana portion contains the texts with notation. A sama song has different parts such as-prastava, udgitha, pratihara, upadrava and nidhana and all of these parts used to be sung by the priests, sometimes together and the other time specially recited by the one priest accordingly. And certain changes are introduced into the text of the song before it is actually sung under-Vikara (the change in a word, e.g. agna changed into ognai), Vislesana (a word broken up into parts, e.g. vitaye broken into voi and toyayi), Vikarsana (lengthening the vowel of the word), Abhyasa (repetition of a word of the song), Virama (pause in the singing of a word), and Stobha (adding some meaningless but interjectional word to the song which is not forming a part of the text but expressive of joy).

Sama music was written in a notation of its own which was numerical. The scale of Sama was a descending one, starting from ma, e.g. ma, ga, re, sa, ni, dha, pa. Here it proves that all the seven notes were in use in Vedic times, Though, the names were different, ma was krusta (madhyama), ga was prathama (gandhara), re was dvitiya (rishabha), sa was tritiya (sadaja), ni was chaturtha (nisada), dha was mandra (dhaivata), and pa was atisvara (panchama) and it appears that all seven notes of the musical scale were discovered by that time. These notes were indicated by the letters 1, 2, 3, 4, 5, 6, 7. Certain devices for lengthening a note were also introduced. A perfect system of chirognomy was also developed by the singers of Sama music. Sama-Vedic notation was the earliest one that was ever developed. The Encyclopaedia Britannica rightly says; 'It is probable that the earliest attempts at notation were made by the Hindus and Chinese from whom the principle was transferred to Greece'.[1]

The Brahmanas, Aranyakas, Sutras, Pratishakhyas and Shiksas contain various references to the music of the ancient times. From these references, it is clear that music had evolved a good deal during this period which may be said to extend from 1,000 B.C. to 600 B.C.

In Samavidhana Brahmana, we get a reference to the seven yamas or notes of the scale. The Taittiriya-Brahmana mentions tunava, shankha, dundubhi and vina. The Taittiriya-Brahmana (III, 9, 14) says that hundred cart-loads of presents were offered to the musicians. This shows the high esteem in which a musician was held at that time. The Satpatha brahmana says that many vinas were played together and the leader of the ensemble of the vinas was called Vina ganagit.

Murchana of the modal shift of scales had also developed by this time. Satapatha Brahmana clearly mentions the Uttara-murchana (XIII, 4, 2, 8; XIII, 4, 2, 11, and XIII, 4, 3, 14).

The Aitreyaranyaka compares the man-made vina to the human body which it calls the divine vina. It gives a description of all the parts of vina which was still a bow-shaped harp. In Sankhayana Srauta Sutra (XVII, 1-3) we get a detailed description of the hundred-stringed vina. In Latyayana Srauta Sutra (IV, 2, 1-10), we get a description of Alabu-vina. Alabu means gourd. This shows that in the vina, gourd had come to be used by this time as a resonator. We also find references in these sutras to kanda-vina which was played with a plectrum and picchora which was a wind instrument.

Some of the Pratisakhyas also contain references to music. The rkpratisakhya mentions the three registers of the voice which it calls mandra(lower register), Madhya (middle register), and uttama(higher register). It also mentions the main physiological organs by means of which the notes in these registers are produced. The notes in the mandra register are produced mainly by lungs, those in the madhya register are produced mainly through the throat, and those in the uttama or taar register are produced mainly through the head. It appears from the commentary of Uvata on the 45th sutra of this pratisakhya that flat and sharp notes were recognized by this time.

The three tempos, viz, vilambita(slow), madhyama(medium), and druta(fast) are also mentioned in this pratisakhya. They were called vritis in the Pratisakhya period.

Puspasutra which is a Pratisakhya of Samaveda contains a good deal of information on Vedic music. According to Dr. Galand, the Puspasutra

Pratisakhya was written in about 900 B.C. it mentions differences in the rendering of Sama-Vedic music in the different schools of Sama-Veda and also many graces like atikarma, uduha, karsana, abhigata, udgata etc.

We notice in this period the gradual evolution of folk music into formalistic, systematic art music. Folk music is generally confined to three to five notes. Sama-Vedic music was also generally confined to three to five notes. It is mainly in these ways that formalized music was developed out of folk music in the Vedic period. Though, all the seven notes were isolated and recognized in course of time in the Vedic period, yet in the entire Sama-Veda, there are very few hymns which use six or seven notes.

The Vedic period analyses the entire music into seven categories. These are called (i) Archika (consisted of one note only), (ii) Gathika (consisted of two notes and was sung usually in praise of some king or feudal lord or on who paid for a particular sacrifice), (iii) Samika (consisted of three notes), (iv) Svarantara (consisted of four notes), (v) Odava (consisted of five notes), (vi) Sadava (consisted of six notes), (vii) Sampurna (consisted of seven notes). At first, the word yama was used for a note. Later, in the Pratisakhya and Siksa period, the note was called svara. The names of the svaras were changed into sadja, rsabha, gandhara, madhyama, panchama, dhaivata, nisada and their solfa names were used as sa, re, ga, ma, pa, dha, ni.

This classification shows that there were three stages in the development of Sama-Vedic music. At the first stage, it employed only three notes. In the next stage, it employed four to five notes. In the final stage, it employed six to seven notes. That is why there are extremely few hymns of the Shadava and Sampurna type in Sama-Veda.The first note in this notation was the key note of the hymn. This note went on changing from hymn to hymn. This contained the germ of the murchana developed later by Bharata.

There was Vriti (rhythm and tempo) in the song, but no system of tala was developed. Simple ornamentation was developed. The chief ornamentations were prenkha (lengthening a note upto two matras), namana (sounding notes in very quick succession, something like the modern ghasita), karsana (passing from one note to another without a break, like the minda), vinata (sounding notes in quick succession in reverse order like the modern ultighasita), atyutkarma (sounding notes in a certain definite order, e.g., sa, ni, dha, ni, like an alamkara) & samprasarana (a small tana like ga,re,sa, ni).The notes of the scale were associated with the middle lines of the fingers of the right hand, and in singing, the thumb or the index finger moved quickly on these lines as the various notes were used. The use of the hand was known as Gatra-Vina.

Post – Vedic Period 600 B.C. to 800 A.D.

The Epic Period- about 700 B.C. to about 150 A.D. Epics are of the great importance to the Vedas. And for the same two Epics are -the "Ramayana" and "Mahabharata".

Ramayana

The Ramayana was composed in Sanskrit by the great poet, Valmiki. It gives a description of the life and exploits of Rama, the son of King Dashratha of Ayodhya, a kingdom in the north of India.

The Ramayana of Valmiki is pre-Budhistic. According to western scholars, the main portion of the Ramayana was composed by about 600 B.C. and additions were made till about 300 or 200 A.D. Music had become fairly developed during this age. Classical music was called Sama-gita or Gandharva. The word atodya which is a blanket term for all kinds of instrumental music occurs in Sundara-kanda (10, 49); there were professional musicians whose services could be requisitioned at any time on payment. There is a reference to the seven (suddha) Jatis (Balakanda 4, 8 and Uttarkanda 94, 2). Jatis were the matrix of the later Ragas. The word vina and tantri occur at many places. Murchana or the modal shift of notes had already been discovered in the Brahman period and there is a reference to it in the Ramayana also (Balakanda 4, 10 and Uttarakanada 93, 13). Karana has been mentioned in Uttarakanda (71, 15). It was in fast tempo. We get a reference to Vipanci-vina in Sundarkanda (10, 41). It was a vina of nine strings and only great experts could play on it successfully.[1]

Among wind instruments we have a reference to Venu (flute) in Kinskindha-kanda (30, 50) and Vamsa which also means flute (in Sundara-kanda). Conch (sankha) was frequently blown on auspicious occasions and at the time of war. In the Ramayana age, there were many varieties of percussion instruments. There was the dundubhi (Yudha-kanda 46, 39) which was what is now popularly known as naggara or nagada,bheri, a kind of mridanga, the right side of which was struck with a stick and the left with hand, mrdanga and a panava (Yudha-kanda 44, 12)- a kind of mridanga in which there was a hole in the middle of the body of the instrument, and three strings were laid from one side to the other, pataha (Sundara-kanda 10, 39)- an instrument like

---

the modern dholaka, dimdima (Sundara-kanda 10, 44) like the damaru but a little smaller than it, adambara (Sundarakanda 11, 6) a kind of mardala or mridanga. Technical terms like kala, matra, samya, pramana, laya and tala, all pertaining to the playing of percussion instruments are also found in the Ramayana.

A study of Ramayana shows that Indian music had developed a great deal in this age. A whole science of music known as Gandharava had come into existence. The singing of jatis was in vogue. Kusilavas (ballad singers) and other professional musicians were very much in demand. Music played an important part in the life of the people. It was used at the time of religious service, in war, on the occasion of festivals, on auspicious occasions, in the courts of kings, in dramas, and the daily life of people. When Rama had to go on exile, messengers were sent to call Bharata to Ayodhya. When he came near Ayodhya, he found that Ayodhya which used to resound with bheri, mridanga, vina etc. day and night was plunged in unusual silence (Ayodhya-kanda 71, 29) and therefore, feared that something ominous has befallen the city.

Performers received high fees and rich gifts from the kings. When Kusa and lava, the two young musicians sang to Rama a portion of the Ramayana at the time of the Asvamedha sacrifice, he was greatly delighted with their performance and asked Bharata to pay 18,000 gold coins to each of them and added that over and above this fee, other presents may be offered to them according to their choice (Uttarakanda 94, 17-

Ravanahatha

18). There were professional bards known as suta, magadha and bandi.

The knowledge of music was widespread. Ravana the demon-leader was proficient in music. The Ravanahatha (ravana hasta veena) is a bowed fiddle popular in Western India. It is also known as Ravanhatha.[1]

Mahabharata

The next important itihasa (epic) is Mahabharata. It is said that it consisted of 24,000 verses. Additions were made time after time until it swelled to one lac verses. C.V. Vaidya is of the opinion that the main theme of the mahabharata was composed soon after the war between the Kauravasa and Pandavas, but Suta narrated it later on. Lassen thinks that the main portion of the Mahabharata was completed in about 400-450 B.C. and it took its present shape much later. The date of the Mahabharata as given by MacDowell is roughly between 500 B.C. and 450 A.D.[2]

We do not find so many references to music in the Mahabharata as in the Ramayana. That may partly be due to the fact that it was an age of conflict and war and music flourishes mostly during peace. Still, there are sufficient evidences in this epic to show that music occupied a very prominent place in the life of the people. It is said in Adi-parva (ch. 70) that Kaca entertained Devayani by singing, dancing and playing the instruments. The word Gandharva occurs in this book in the sense of the science and art of music.

In Dronaparva, we find a reference to the following instruments:-Mridanga, jharkhara, bheri, panava, anaka, gomukha, adambara, sankha, dundubhi.

In Santi-parva, there is reference to vina and venu (ch. 52, 4-5). In Virata-parva (ch. 70, 33-34), there is a reference to Kansya. Some of these instruments have been referred to, at many places.

Of these, vina was a stringed instrument, mridanga, jharjhara or jharjhari, bheri, panava, anaka, adambara and dundubhi were instruments of the membranophonic class (drum class), sankha and venu were wind instruments. Gomukha was possibly a cow-faced horn or trumpet. Kansya was the cymbal.

Training in music was considered to be an important part of the culture of a person. Arjuna had learned the art of singing, dancing and playing an instrument, and when he was in disguise in Virat Nagar, he taught these arts to Uttara, the daughter of the king of Virat Nagar (Virata-parva ch. III).

During this age, there were dance and music institutions in which girls used to receive instruction in music and dance during the day. Matsya-raja, for instance, had built such an institution (Virata-parva, ch. 25.3).We, therefore, find that classical music was assiduously practiced during the Mahabharata age, and it had an important place in the life of the people.[1]

Photo : Eon Image, Image date: ca. 1913

Mahabharata used the term gandharva instead of sangeet. The epic therefore referred to a more specific kind of music. Musicology or the science of music was called gandharva-shastra. Super human beings called Gandharvas were the expert practitioners of this music. Both gandharvas and their consorts, the apsaras, were experts in singing, playing musical instruments and dancing.

Arjuna, had learnt these musical arts from Chitrasen gandharva. Kings maintained their own music schools to train princesses and their maids in the performing arts. The names of the seven basic musical notes (shadja) have been clearly mentioned in the Mahabharata, which was composed around 400 BC. The epic therefore bears testimony to the long living tradition of Indian Classical music.

Music in the Buddhist and Jain Sources

Music was cultivated by Buddhism also. The general belief that music was taboo among the Buddhists is not borne out by facts. Lalita-vistara which gives an account of the Buddha's life says that he, as a prince, had received training in playing vina, singing and dance.[1] Buddha was not against music as such, but only against sensual music, against 'Samaja' in which people exulted in drunken revelry. Such kind of music has been denounced by Manusmrti also. The Jataka tales which describe the past lives of the Buddha contain many references to music. Scenes from some of the Jatakas have been depicted in reliefs on the stone walls around the stupas of Bharahuta and Sanchi. The stupas are said to have been built in the 3rd or 2nd century B.C. Scenes from the Jatakas could have been depicted in the reliefs of these stupas only if they had acquired sufficient reputation as authentic and had been fairly known to the people. The Jatakas must have existed a hundred or fifty years earlier in order to have acquired popularity.[2]

In Dadhivahana Jataka, it is related that a Brahmin named Saka had presented a drum to his brother who was living on a hill, saying,

---

'If u beat on one side of a drum, your enemies would run away; if u beat on the other side they would become your friends.[1]

It is said in one of the Jatakas that Bodhisattva in a previous life was an excellent musician. His name was guttila. He was employed as court-musician by Brahmadatta, the king of Kasi. A musician named Musila; hearing of his reputation came from Ujjayani to learn music from him. Guttila in all sincerity taught him all he knew. One day the king arranged a musical gathering in his palace in which both the musicians were asked to perform. The king, considering Guttila to be a better musician awarded him a present which was twice as much in cost as that offered to Musila. Musila could not bear this. He fell out with his teacher. Their quarrel was referred to the king who ruled that he would hold a competition between the two in order to decide the issue. Guttila had become old and was doubtful whether he would emerge successful if a competition was held. He retired to a forest and there prayed to Indra for his success. Indra granted him a boon saying, 'when u sing before the king, go on breaking one string after another of your vina. The vina could go on repeating the music even when the six strings are broken, and there would not be the slightest lapse in the sweetness of your song. This is a feat which your rival would not be able to perform.' Guttila returned to the court and defeated Musila in the competition.[2]

We learn two things from this story. Songs were sung in accompaniment to the vina, and the vina in those ancient times had seven strings. Vina in the ancient times was like a harp. It was played on open strings. The instrumentalists of those times had developed excellent plucking technique. Guttila had, in addition, practised the art of producing on a single string the notes of other strings by damping aliquot parts of it. So he could go on breaking string after string and could play the melody. The string that finally remained was the longest and so it was possible to produce the notes of the other strings by the above method. It was this technique that enabled Guttila to defeat his rival.

Bheri or drum was very much in use. It was used in battle and in announcing the orders of the king.

The Mahajanaka Jataka refers to the four great sounds (parma maha sbda) that were conferred as a honour by the king on great persons. These sounds were of drum, horn, gong and cymbals. These were two chariots. The first one was un-occupied. This was followed by musicians who sounded the above instruments so that the sound produced was like the roar of the sea.

After this was the chariot in which was seated the personage who was honoured. The chariot moved slowly round the palace and upon what was known as the 'kettele-drum road' (bheri-marga). The fact that music instruments were selected as symbols of honour goes to show the great esteem in which music was held during those times.

Playing of instruments was a respectable profession. It is recorded that Bodhisattva himself was a professional player of bheri (a drum like the modern dholaka) and shankha (conch) in two lives.[1]

Sculpture showing music in Buddhist period
Photograph : Benoy K. Behl

In processions, all kinds of instruments were carried and played in the last chariot.[1]We learn from Mahasara and Takkariya Jataka that every king had his court musician.

There are many references to vina in Milindapanha, a dialogue between a Buddhist monk and a Greek king, Menander (about 100 B. C.). Asvaghosa, the great Buddhist poet travelled from place to place with a band of musicians, singing devotional songs composed in honour of Buddha, and spreading the message of Buddhism.[2]

Bow shaped vina was very much in use in early buddhist period. Its hollow belly was known as doni. It had seven strings (sattatanti) which were one above the other and extended from the arm to the belly. The following varieties of the vina are mentioned in the Buddhist book, viz; Parivadini, Vallaki,Mahati, Nakuli, Kachhapi and Tumbuvina. A few other instruments mentioned in the Jatakas are adambara, anaka, samatala (cymbals), kumbhathana (ther modern name is jalataranga), sankha (conch). Music was fairly widely cultivated. The Budhhist book Avadanasataka says that there were five hundred musicians in Sravasti alone. (Excavation in Sahet-mahet in Bahraich District (U.P.) has proved that this was the ancient town of Sravasti).[1]

Music had an honoured place among the jains also. We find the names of all the seven notes in Sthananga Sutra (about second century B.C.) and other important books that contain information on music are Rajaprasniya Sutra, nandi and Anuyogadvara. The effects of the various musical notes have been elaborately described in Sthananga Sutra. There is also a reference to the three gramas or foundational tone systems, viz; sadja, gandhara and madhyama. The murchanas(shift sclaes) given under three gramas do not correspond with the murchanas given in othe books. Sthananga Sutra also discusses the qualities of good music.

The Nandi Sutra mentions a number of musical instruments, viz; Maddala (mardala), Kadava, Jhallari, Hudukka, Kansala, Kahala, Talima, Vamsa, Sankha, Panava etc.

Ancient Music in Tamil Sources

We have references to music in early Tamil literature also. In the Tamil books Purananuru and Puttupattu which were written between A.D. 100-200, the drum has been mentioned in terms of great respect. It enjoyed almost the same respect as a deity. Three kinds of drums have been mentioned in the above books, viz; (1) the battle drum, (2) the judgment drum and (3) the sacrificial drum. Its capture was considered to be the defeat of the army itself.

The Paripadal (About 100 to 200 A.D.) mentions the seven padai which were the ancient Dravidian modes. The Yala was the most important musical instrument of the south. Some of the varieties of Yala had one thousand strings. It was like a bow shaped harp.

The most important book which contains a good deal of the information on music in the south is Silappadikaram. This is a drama in Tamil written in 2nd century A.D. the title means 'the story that centers around a Silambu or Anklet. It has sic cantos on music, and gives an elaborate description of the dance and music prevalent in that age. It shows to what great extent music had developed among the Dravidians in the ancient past. Isa is the technical term used for music. Four varieties of pans or ragas were developed, appropriate to each of the four regions into which the Tamil land was divided. Besides vocal music, the Tamil land had developed Vina, Yala, Flute and Drum in instrumental music. The Yala was distinguished by the number of strings it contained. The Flute was classified into five types-made of bamboo, sandalwood, bronze, red catechu and ebony. There were thirty-one kinds of percussion instruments. The suddha scale of the ancient Tamils was like Harikamboji of Karnatala music or Khamaja of Hindustani music.[1]

Tivakaram, a Jain lexicon of the 3rd century A.D. gives a lot of information on Dravidian music. According to it, two kinds of ragas had developed by that time—the heptatonic, using all the seven notes, and the transilient or hexatonic and pentatonic i.e., using six or five notes. The former, i.e., the complete mode was called pan and the latter, i.e., the transilient mode was called tiram. The book also refers to 22 strutis which it terms mantra. The use of the word mantra for sruti is found in Silappadikaram also. The names of the seven musical notes, the seven Dravidian modes, called palai, four kinds of yala and the name of 29 pans are mentioned in Tivakaram. All this goes to prove that musical culture had fairly developed in the Tamil land as early as the 2nd and 3rd century or the Christian era.

Music as Described in Natya-Sastra
(The Development of Gandharva Music)

The oldest book available on dramaturgy and musical theory is the Natya-Sastra of Bharata.

The main portion of the book was written about 200 or 100 B.C. additions were made later. Kalidasa mentions Bharata by name 'Munina Bharatena' in verse 18, Act.-II of Vikramorvarsi. Therefore, he must have flourished much earlier than Kalidasa. Natya-sastra acquired the present shape between 200 and 300 A.D. bharata who was known as Vrddha Bharata or Adi Bharata was the main writer of the book. He was the first person to systematize the science of dramaturgy and he acquired such importance that Bharata became a common name for an actor. His followers made considerable addition to the book. The word Bharata has been used in plural at places in Natya-Sastra itself. The drama Surya-Sankalpodya says that Bharata became as acrostic word, bha standing for bhava (emotion), ra standing for raga (musical delineation) and ta standing for tala (time cycle). Bharata, therefore came to mean one who combined within himself a deep knowledge of Bhava, Raga and Tala. The main theme of Natya-Sastra is dramaturgy, but it also discusses certain fundamental principles of music and applied music i.e., music as used for the purpose of drama.[1]

The word 'Gandharva' was used in two senses—general and specific. In a general sense, all formalized music was known as Gandharava. In the specific sense, Gandharva meant music that was sung or played for adrsta phala i.e., religious merit, for praising the gods and acquiring salvation. Bharata has used the word Gandharava in his specific sense. It is this kind of music that he has described in Natya-Sastra. The music that was sung or played merely for entertainment has been designated as Gana by Bharata. He has used this kind of music only in certain parts of the drama where the main purpose is entertainment. Six chapters of this book (ch.28-33) deal mainly with music. He discusses the two fundamental tonal systems sadja grama, and madhyama grama, which were the foundation of all scales. By an experiment, he demonstrates the interval of the various notes from one another measured by shrutis or microtones intervening between them. He also gives the murchana or scales obtained by the transposition of the keynote.

The most ancient type of stylized music in India was known as Jati. We find a reference to seven Jatis in Valmiki's Ramayana. Bharata mentions eighteen jatis. Of these eighteen jatis, seven were derived from the Sadja grama, and the remaining eleven were derived from the Madhyama grama. Four Jatis of Sadja grama and three of Madhyama grama were known as Suddha Jatis. The rest were obtained by the fusion of two or more jatis from each grama. These were known as vikrta Jatis (i.e., modified Jatis). Valmiki mentions only seven jatis which were obviously the seven suddha

———————————————

or unmodified jatis. It appears that the additional eleven were developed during a long course of time.

Bharata has classified all musical instruments into four classes:--

1. Tala or stringed instruments e.g., vina.
2. Susira or instruments with holes i.e., wind instruments, e.g., flute.
3. Avanaddha, i.e., instruments covered with skin e.g., mridanga.
4. Ghana or instruments made of brass or wood to mark time, e.g. cymbals.

This classification is perfectly scientific and exhaustive. When all kinds of musical instruments were collected in Europe and a museum was formed at Brussels, the problem that arose was how to classify such bewildering variety of instruments. Such was the scientific character and exhaustive nature of Bharata's classification that they ultimately seized upon this classification and adopted it in to. The following quotation from F.W. Galpin's 'Text Book of European Instruments' will bear this out.

"In 1877, when the Museum of Musical Instruments was formed in connection with the Conservatoire Royal de Musique at Brussels, with M. Victor Mahillon as Curator and M. Gevaert as Director, this fourfold division (viz; tata, susira, avanaddha and ghana) was adopted".[1]

Bharata mentions kutapa (ensemble of musical instruments to be played together) and gives two important varieties of it, viz; tata kutapa, i.e., ensemble of stringed instruments, and avanaddha kutapa, i.e., ensemble of membranophonic instruments. These formed the ancient Indian orchestra.

He also gives a detailed description of vina, and the technique of playing it, and of flute, and the method of playing it. He devotes one whole chapter to avnaddha vadyas or membranophonic instruments and describes in detail the making of these instruments, particularly of mrdanga, panava, dardura and the technique of playing them.

He gives a detailed description of seven kinds of complex tala structures, viz; madraka, dvikalamadraka-aparantaka, ullopyaka, prakari, ovenaka, rovindaka and uttaragitaka. He gives a very comprehensive treatment of dhruva songs which were mostly sung in connection with the various acts of the drama. The dhruva song was a very specialized vocal composition and had as many as eighteen sub-divisions. He also describes the metres of the dhruva songs in detail.

Bharata gives breath-taking details pertaining to stage, décor, acting and dance. So far as music is concerned, he has written mostly on applied music, i.e., music as applied to the histrionic art, but has also discussed the fundamental general principles of Gandharva Music.

Music in The Puranic Sources

The Puranas also contain a good deal of information on Indian music. They give mostly information on creation, dissolution and recreation, divine genealogies, ages of Manus, genealogies of kings, philosophy, yoga etc. but some of them contain information on poetry and music also. They are veritable ancient encyclopaedias giving information practically on all subjects known to ancient India. Haraprasada Sastri rightly says:

"Anything old may be the subject of a Purana,
and it covers all the aspects of life."[1]

There are eighteen Maha-Puranas and eighteen Upa-Puranas according to the traditional view. The various Puranas were compiled in different periods. The earliest of them was contemporaneous with the Mahabharata. Information on music is mostly available in Vayu-Purana, Markandeya Purana and Vishnu-Dharamottara Purana. There is some information on music in Harivamsa also. Harivamsa is, really speaking, a supplement to the Mahabharata. Some include it among the Puranas.

The date of Harivamsa is generally considered to be 200 B.C. to 200 A.D. harivamsa refers to Sama music and the ancient classical music of India which is designated as Gandharva. The Grama Ragas have been specifically mentioned in this book. Some of the important musical instruments are also referred to. There is also an interesting description of Hallisa or Hallisaka which was a folk group dance. This seems to have developed into the Rasa dance which continues till today in Vraja (Mathura and the neighbouring region)[2]

A good deal of praise has been bestowed in Harivamsa on a type of musical performance known as Chalikya.

It was a Gandharva type of singing accompanied by a number of musical instruments. It is said that the six Grama-ragas were implicitly involved in it, and it could be acquired by very arduous practice. Only Krishna and a few gandharvas knew how to give a performance of Chalikya.

_____

There were two types of Chalikya—group Chalikya and solo Chalikya. It was a type of music accompanied with dance and acting. In later times, the words Chalika and Calita were also used for Chalikya. Vina, venu (flute) and mridanga were the instruments of accompaniment that were generally used in Chalikya music. Krishna was said to be the inventor of this type of music. He was also the inventor of Hallisaka group dance which developed into Rasa. In Harivamsa, Krishna is mainly the center of various musical activities.

Three gramas, viz; Sadja grama, Madhyama grama and Gandhara Grama are mentioned in Harivamsa.

The following musical instruments were in use in that period—vina, vallaki, mahati, among stringed instruments—panava, dardura, anaka, muraja, mrdanga and bheri among membranophonic instruments, and among wind instruments.[1]

The Vayu Purana which was written in about 500 A.D., mentions all the seven swaras, three gramas viz; Sadja, Madhyama and Gandhara together with their murchanas (shift scales), and the tanas (elaboration of notes) pertaining to the three gramas. It also gives an elaborate description of varnas (repetition of the same notes after pauses, and arrangements of notes in ascending, descending and mixed order), alamkaras or combination of notes in a definite order used in music and songs of various types particularly madraka, aparantaka and uttara gitas. The following musical instruments have been mentioned in this Purana—mardala, dundubhi, ghanta, jharjhara, sankha, pataha, bheri, dimadima, gomukha and tumburu-vina.[1]

In Markandeya Purana (about 900 A.D.) also, there is a reference to the seven notes, grama-ragas, murchanas, seven varieties of vocal music, three varieties of laya (rhythm and tempo), 49 tanas and the four varieties of musical instruments (stringed, membranophones, wind and cymbals). The following instruments are particularly mentioned—vina, venu, dardura, panava, mridanga, pataha, anaka and dundubhi.

Vishnudharmottara, among all the Puranas contains the most numerous references to music. It describes the seven notes, the three gramas, the murchanas assigned to each grama, the tanas pertaining to each grama, the various alamkaras, varieties of gita (songs), laya (rhythm and tempo), and tala (time cycle), the four types of musical instruments and music as applied to drama.

Music in Kalidasa's Works

There are references to music in many of the works of Kalidasa. The words samgita (music), gana (song), gandharva (science of music, classical music), mridanga, muraja (a kind of drum), vina occur at many places in Kalidasa's works.

Both the words vina and murchana occur in verse 26 in Uttara-megha. Kalidasa says that Yaksini who was keenly feeling the pangs of saparation from her lord, the Yaksa, tried to tone down the intensity of her feeling by playing on her vina a song which she had composed and which contained the name of the Yaksa. She required a particular scale for the particular

---

melody of the song, but such was the intensity of her feeling that though she had herself tuned her vina in a particular scale, she would forget the scale when actually starting to play the song. In this context, Kalidasa uses the word 'murchana' for the shifting scale. Murchana was a scale which gave a particular series of notes in ascending and descending order. This was a model shift executed for getting particular notes for playing of singing a particular tune requiring those notes. Murchana started from the time of Samaveda and continued till the 14th or 15th century when it was displaced by Mela. Kalidasa knew the use of murchana very well.[1]

At another place in Kumarsambhava, (sarga viii, verse 85), Kalidasa says that kinnaras awakened Siva in the morning by singing gita-mangala (auspicious song) in kaisika set in a particular murchana. Here Kalidasa has used the word murchana again. He has also used two other technical words, viz; kaisika and gita-mangala. While gita-mangala ordinarily means an auspicious song, it also means a particular kind of musical composition containing benedictory ideas and set in kaisika tune and either in nihsaru tala or mangala meter. Gita-mangala or mangala-gita was a very ancient musical composition. It was generally sung by bards and minstrels. It was in use in the Mahabharata age, as we find a reference to this in Dronaparva. Sarngadeva has included mangalacara and mangala-gita or gita-mangala among the Viprakrna prabandhas and says that such a song was sung in kaisika raga and nihsaru tala or mangala chanda. Kaisika was a very ancient grama-raga and was in use even in the time of the Mahabharata. The fact that Kalidasa uses the word 'gita-mangala' in connection with kaisika in Kumara-sambhava goes to prove that he is using 'gita-mangala' in this technical sense, and that he was aware of such a composition. In Vikramovarsiyam, Kalidasa refers to Kakubha raga.

In Malavikagnimitra, we come across many musical terms. Ganadasa, the dance teacher says to the king (Act II)

"Deva, Sarmisthayah krtilayamadhya chatuspada"—"Sir, the krti of Sarmistha is in madhyalaya and is catuspada"

In above sentence, we get three musical terms viz;

(1) Krti which means musical composition. The word is still used in the same sense in Karnataka music

(2) Madhyalaya which means medium tempo

(3) Chatushpada which means a composition having four parts or lines.

In the same act, we get a few more musical terms. Malavika appears before the king, and the poet says about her:

"Upaganam krtva catuspada vastu gayati"

Here again, we get two musical terms, viz; upagana and catuspada vastu. Upagana or upohana means a musical prelude, a preparatory tune, a short alapa which is sung by way of prelude before the main piece is taken up for rendering. We have seen what catuspada means. 'Vastu' is another word for a musical piece or a composition. In some versions of Malavikagnimitra, Ganadasa requests the king to witness the chalika performance of Sarmistha. In the first act of this drama, the word 'calita' occurs which according to the commentator, Katayavema, refers to calita dance. Calita and chalika refer to the same dance. This word occurs in Harivamsa also. Calita, chalika or chalikya was a highly developed classical dance which was accompanied by vina, venu (flute) and mridanga, in which a song was accompanied by acting expressive of the sentiment of the song.[1]

In Malavikagnimitra, Kalidasa refers to mayuri marjana of puskara. Puskara was a generic word for drum in ancient times. Marjana was the ancient word for tuning of drums. In ancient times, three drums were played with vocal and instrumental music. These days only two drums are played e.g. either the tabla or the two faces of mridanga. Mayuri marjana is a technical term for a particular type of tuning of the drum. In Mayuri marjana, the left side of the drum was tuned to the note gandhara, the right to sadja, and the urdhvaka or the upper drum was tuned to madhyama.[2]

Kalidasa says that Mayuri marjana of mridanga resembles the thunder of clouds and is, therefore, dear to the mayura, the peacock. The commentator, the Katayavema adds that because it was 'mayurapriya' dear to mayura or peacock, so it was called mayuri marjana.

In the drama Vikramorvarsiyam, Kalidasa mentions in the 4th act many ancient musical compositions like Dvipadika, Jambhalika, Khandadhara, Carcari, Bhinnaka, Khandaka, Khuraka etc. They were mostly musical compositions in Prakrta. Sarngadeva says in his Samgita-Ratnakara that carcari or caccari was the name of a tala in which compositions were sung in raga Hindol at the time of the spring festival (vasantotsava). This composition was named after the tala. The modern holi festival is a remnant of the ancient vasantotsava. There were sixteen matras or beats in the ancient carcari tala. In modern times, Holi is sometimes sung in Chachara but this is a tala of fourteen beats.[3]

In Sakuntala drama, we get reference to Varna in the technical sense-

"*Jane tatrabhavati hansapadika varnaparicayam karotiti (Act V) i.e.*
"believe hansapadika is practicing varna."

Among instruments, we find in his works references to vina, vallaki vina, venu, sankha and drums like muraja, mardala and mridanga. According to Abhinavagupta, Kalidasa wrote Ghatakarpara-kulaka on which he has written a commentary. Abhinava says that this was a gita-kavya which was to be presented on the stage with music and dance. Kulaka is a kind of gita-kavya. Abhinava mentions that the Ghatakarpara-kulaka is Kalidasa's composition. This goes to show that Kalidasa was not only a connoisseur of music but also an expert in musical composition.

Musical references in other musical epics

In the beginning of the Christian era, some new ragas and gitis were included in the category of formalized regional (desi) type of music which flourished side by side of the gandharva type of music, the basis of which is to be found in Bharata's Natya-sastra, and fully delineated in Matanga's Brihaddesi of the 5th-7th century A.D.

The gramaragas had their origin in the jatis or jatiragas, having their nucleus in the two gramas, sadja and madhyama, ("jati-sambhutatvat gramaragani"). The gandhara-grama fell out of practice at that time. Later on different kinds of mixed (misra anga) ragas evolved from the gramaragas. The mixture of the Aryan and the non-Aryan tunes (ragas) commenced from the 3rd-5th century and continued up to the 12th-13th century A.D., and this admixture is evident in the works like Brhaddesi, Sangita-samayasara and Sangita-ratnakara. The Turkish, Scythian and Persian tunes were also adopted in the stock of Indian classical music,

making them suitable to the taste and temperament of the changing society. The fusion took place mainly during the periods, 5th-7th and 11th-13th centuries A.D. The ragas were characterized by ten essentials like Sonant, Consonant, Dissonant, etc., and there was a perfect consonance (svara-samvada) between the notes, first and fourth and first and fifth, as was vogue in the ancient Greek music.

From the statement of Narada's naradisiksa of the 1st century A.D., we come to know that the microtonal units (srutis) were in use in both the gandharva and formalized desi types of music. The microtonal units or microtones are the minute perceptible tones. Bharata has analyzed the seven laukika tones, sadja, etc. into twenty-two minutes tones (srutis) on the basis of the genus-species or jati-vyakti (cause-effect) theory, as devised by Narada.

The period covering the 5th-7th century to the 13th century A.D. can be considered as the period of renaissance in the domain of Indian music, because during this period many old and new ragas came into being from different sources, and they enriched the treasury of Indian classical music. The ragagitis were known by their respective ragas during Matanga's time, and many new ragas and gitis evolved from them. The ragas were determined by different murchanas, which were again replaced by melas or thatas or melakartas in the 16th-17th century A.D. The intuitive authors and artists of music considered the ragas as the living embodiments of divine spirit, and they made them surcharged with aesthetic or emotional sentiments and feelings (rasa and bhava), composed the dhyana-formulas, and painted their exquisite colourful pictures (ragamala), which came to be known as the visualized music.

Well has it been said by Prof. O.C. Gangoly in this connection that:

"*Each raga and melody was then dedicated to its own theme, its ethos, its presiding genus, its devatas. And it was by the prayer of the adept musician, the singer, or the interpreter, who had to immerse in the theme and identify himself with it, that the devatas—the spirit of the raga was made visible (murtimanta) in the symphonic form-- the nadamaya rupa, and thus they used to visualize the image of the raga in ecstatic vision.*"

Different kinds of musical phrases (sthaya) and compositions (prabandha) were in use even at the beginning of the Christian era, and they have been described in Bharata's Natyasastra in connection with the classical dramatic performances. Matanga, Parsvadeva and Sarangdeva have elaborated them in a systematic and scientific way in their respective works.

The development of classical music in South-India is also interesting. In ancient times, there was no such artificial line of demarcation, dividing the music of India into Northern and Southern categories. Probably during the 14th-16th century A.D. Madhava-Vidyaranya (1302-1387 A.D.), Ramamatya (1550 A.D.) and Pundarika Vitthala (1590 A.D.) flourished, and propagated the genus-species (janya-janaka) principle of the ragas, with mukhari as the standard scale (suddha-mela). The system of the South Indian music gradually began to take new shape, and afterwards became different from that of the North Indian music. Afterwards, Somanath (1609 A.D.), Govinda Dixit (1614 A.D.) and Venkatamakhi (1620 A.D.) flourished with a new vision. The introduction of the seventy-two melakartas by Govinda Diksit and Venkatamakhi brought into being an altogether different mode in the South Indian music. But it should be mentioned in this connection that in spite of the introduction of the seventy-two melakartas or thatas, only nineteen out of them were practiced during Venkatamakhi's time. The tonal forms of most of the ragas of the South Indian system were also different from those of the North. The various padam, krti or kirtanam, varnam, ragamalika, pallavi, contributed by Purandaradasa, ksetrajna, Tayagaraja, Syama Sastri, Muthusvami Diksitar, Svati Tirunal and others, enriched the South Indian music.

Kudumiyamalai Inscription

The musical inscription at Kudumiyamalai throws a flood of light on the ancient music of India. Kudumiyamalai means literally 'the hill of him who was the sikha'. At Kudumiyamalai is the Sikhanathasvami temple near Melaikkovil in South India. The musical inscription in engraved on a rock on the slope of the hill behind the Sikhanathasvami temple. The engraving has been done in pallava-grantha character. The language used in Sanskrit except in a line at the end which is in Tamil.[1]

The inscription contains quadruple groupings of musical notes pertaining to the seven ancient grama-ragas. Actually there were at first only six grama-ragas, viz;

1.   Sadja-Grama,
2.   Madhyama-Grama,
3.   Pancama,
4.   Sadava,
5.   Sadharita,
6.   Kaisikamadhyama.

A seventh, viz; kaisika was added later on. These were the precursors of modern ragas.

---

1. Indian Music , Page 35

Kudumiyamalai is in Pudukkotai estate in South India. The inscription was composed in 7th century A.D. Mahendra Vikrama Varman I of the Pallavas is believed to be its author. The inscription was discovered in 1904, and was edited by P.R. Bhandarkar in 1914. The inscription is engraved in sa ri ga ma or solfa notation. In the case of each grama-raga, the words 'catusprahara svaragamah' are mentioned. 'Catus' means a group of four, and 'Prahara' means stroke. The various notes are actually engraved in a group of 'four'. The word 'prahara' or stroke shows that these notes were for practice in vina-playing.

As has already been said, next to Samavedic music these grama-ragas were the most ancient music of India. All the seven notes have been used in this inscription. Besides, antaragandhara and kakali-nisada have also been used.

What comprises Indian Music

Indian music is vast section that includes several genre of music and several types of music. If we consider music of India, you can see a wide variety that include folk music, popular music, classical music, pop music, traditional music and many other forms of music. India also has a great musical history that also reflects in the culture as well as tradition of Indians.

Let's have a look to the major forms of Indian music at a glance because only the different forms of the particular parts of a building can tell the whole story.

The two main streams of Indian classical music are:

* *Hindustani classical music, originally from North India*
* *Carnatic music (Karnataka Sangeeth), originally from South India.*

Hindustani Classical Music

Hindustani music is a classical music tradition that goes back to Vedic times, and further developed circa the 13th and 14th centuries AD with Persian influences and from existing religious and folk music. The practice of singing based on notes was popular even from the Vedic times where the hymns in Sama Veda, a sacred text, was sung as Samagana and not chanted. Developing a strong and diverse tradition over several centuries, it has contemporary traditions established primarily in India but also in Pakistan and Bangladesh.

Hidustani Music comprises a magnificent assortment of musical types that cannot be just comprehended in few readings. And when it comes to classical or Hindustani music, the stature even gets elevated to sublime heights. Rooted in the ancient centuries of evolvement, the major vocal forms or styles associated with Hindustani classical music are dhrupad, khayal, and tarana. Other forms include dhamar, trivat, chaiti, kajari, tappa, ashtapadis, thumri, and dadra; each of these forms are legendary in their historical germination.[1]

In Hindustani Music, when we talk about the classical front then the performance usually begins with a slow elaboration of the raga, known as alap. This can range from very long (30-40 minutes) to very short (2-3 minutes) depending on the style and preference of the musician. Once the

---

raga is established, the ornamentation around the mode begins to become rhythmical, gradually speeding up. Finally, the percussionist joins in and the tala is introduced.

When it comes to the semi classical front then there are so many forms in which the time limitation is not a concern. It has more to do with the regional stuff like folk music and different famous styles of different states which entertains the lay crowd. There are many forms of semi classical music like dadra, kajri, chaiti, tappa etc.

When it comes to the light music then it is more of the compositional structure which catches the attention of almost everyone. The execution of light music involves everyone who is listening to it. Bhajans and the light songs fall under this category.

Carnatic music

Carnatic music, also known as karnātaka sangītam is one of the two styles of Indian classical music, the other being Hindustani music. The present form of Carnatic music is based on historical developments. From the several epigraphically inscriptional evidences and other ancient works, the history of classical musical traditions can be traced back about years.

In Carnatic music, the main emphasis is on vocal music; most compositions are written to be sung, and even when played on instruments, they are meant to be performed in a singing style (known as gāyaki). Like Hindustani music, Carnatic music rests on two main elements: raga, the modes or melodic formulae, and tala the rhythmic cycles. Like all art forms in Indian culture, Carnatic Music is believed to have a divine origin – it is believed to have originated from the Devas and

Devis. However, it is also generally accepted that the natural origins of music were an important factor in the development of Carnatic music. Ancient treatises describe the connection of the origin of Swaras to the sounds of animals and birds, and man's keen sense of observation and perception that tried simulating these sounds – after hearing and distinguishing between the different sounds that emanated from bamboo reed when air passes through its hollows, man designed the first flute. In this way, music is venerated as an aspect of the supreme (Nāda Brāhmam). Folk music is also said to have been a natural origin of Carnatic music, with many folk tunes corresponding to certain Carnatic ragas.

Carnatic music is based on music concepts mentioned in Bharata's Natya Shastra. The Natya Shastra mentions many musical concepts (including swara and tala) that continue to be relevant to Carnatic music today.

According to some scholars, Carnatic music shares certain classical music concepts with ancient Tamil music. The concept of Pann is related to Ragas used in Carnatic music. The rhythmic meters found in several musical forms (such as the Tiruppugazh) and other ancient literature, resemble the talas that are in use today.

Both Carnatic and Hindustani music shared a common history. And, as a result of the increasing Persian influence (and as a result of the Islamic conquest) in North India, Hindustani Music started evolving as a separate genre, while Carnatic music was relatively unaffected by these Arabic and Iranian influences. In Carnatic Music (which was based in South India), the pan-Indian bhakti movement laid a substantial basis as far as the use of religious themes are concerned, while major developments also contributed to its divergence from Hindustani music.

Carnatic music saw renewed growth during the Vijayanagar Empire by the Kannada Haridasa movement of Vyasaraja, Purandara Dasa, Kanakadasa and others. Purandara Dasa who is known as the Sangeeta Pitamaha (the grandfather of Carnatic music) laid out the fundamental tenets and framework for teaching Carnatic music. Venkatamakhi is credited with the classification of ragas in the Melakarta System and wrote his most important work; Chaturdandi Prakasika in Sanskrit. Govindacharya expanded the Melakarta Scheme into the Sampoorna raga system, which is the system in common use today.

Even though the earlier writers Matanga, Sarangadeva and others also were from Karnataka, the music tradition was formally named Karnataka Sangeetha when the Vijayanagara Empire was founded.

A unique development in the art of instrumental carnatic music took shape under the patronage of the kings of the Kingdom of Mysore. The composers used to play their compositions on instruments such as the veena, rudra veena, violin, tambura, ghata, flute, mridangam, nagaswara, swarabhat. Some instruments such as harmonium, sitar and jaltarang, though uncommon to the southern region came into use and the English Influence popularised the saxophone and piano. Even royalty of this dynasty were noted composers and proficient in playing musical instruments, solo or in concert with others. Some famous instrumentalists were Veena Sheshanna, Veena Subbanna, T. Chowdiahand others.

Carnatic music is practised and presented today by musicians in concerts or recordings, either vocally or through instruments. Carnatic music itself developed around musical works or compositions of phenomenal composers.

Compositions

In contrast to Hindustani Music of the northern part of India, Carnatic music is taught and learned through compositions, which encode many intricate musical details, also providing scope for free improvisation. Nearly every rendition of a Carnatic music composition is different and unique as it embodies elements of the composer's vision, as well as the musician's interpretation.

A Carnatic composition really has two elements, one being the musical element, the other being what is conveyed in the composition. It is probably because of this fact that most Carnatic music compositions are composed for singing. In addition to the rich musical experience, each composition brings out the knowledge and personality of the composer, and hence the words are as important as the musical element itself. This poses a special challenge for the musicians because rendering this music does not involve just playing or singing the correct musical notes; the musicians are expected to understand what was conveyed by the composer in various languages, and sing musical phrases that act to create the effect that was intended by the composer in his/her composition.

There are many types/forms of compositions. Geethams and Swarajatis (which have their own peculiar composition structures) are principally meant to serve as basic learning exercises, and while there are many other types/forms of compositions (including Padam, Javali and Thillana), the most common forms are the Varnam, and most importantly, the Kriti (or Keerthanam), which are discussed below.

Varnam: This is a special item which highlights everything important about a raga; not just the scale, but also which notes to stress, how to approach a certain note, classical and characteristic phrases, etc. Though there are a few different types of varnams, in essence, they all have a pallavi, an anupallavi, muktayi swaras, a charana, and chittaswaras. They are sung in multiple speeds, and are very good for practice. In concerts, varnams are often sung at the beginning as they are fast and grab the audience's attention.

Kriti: Carnatic songs (kritis) are varied in structure and style, but generally consist of three units:

Pallavi: This is the equivalent of a refrain in Western music, One or two lines.

Anupallavi: The second verse. Also two lines.

Charana: The final (and longest) verse that wraps up the song. The Charanam usually borrows patterns from the Anupallavi. There can be multiple charanas.

This kind of song is called a keerthanam or a Kriti. There are other possible structures for a Kriti, which may in addition include swara passages named chittaswara. Chittaswara consists only of notes, and has no words. Still others have a verse at the end of the charana, called the madhyamakāla. It is sung immediately after the charana, but at double speed.

Carnatic raga elaborations are generally much faster in tempo and shorter. The opening piece is called a Varna, and is a warm-up for the musicians. Devotion and a request for a blessing follow, then a series of inter-changes between ragas (unmetered melody) and talas (the ornamentation, equivalent to the jor). This is inter-mixed with hymns called kritis. This is followed by the pallavi or theme from the raga. Carnatic pieces can also be fixed; these are famous compositions that are popular among those who appreciate Carnatic (especially vocal) music.

Carnatic music is similar to Hindustani music in that it is mostly improvised (see musical improvisation), but it is much more influenced by theory and has stricter rules. It emphasizes the expertise of the voice rather than that of the instruments. Primary themes include Devi worship, Rama worship, descriptions of temples and patriotic songs. Sri Purandara Dasa (1480 – 1564) is known as the father of Carnatic music. Tyagaraja (1759 – 1847), Muthuswami Dikshitar (1776 – 1827) and Syama Sastri (1762 – 1827) are known as Trinity of Carnatic music.

Performers

There have been many great exponents of Hindustani music. Some of them are Allauddin Khan, Vilayat Khan, Bade Ghulam Ali Khan, Abdul Karim Khan, Vasantrao Deshpande, Ustad Amir Khan, Salamat Ali, Mallikarjun Mansur, Omkarnath Thakur, Bismillah Khan, Gangubai Hangal, Bhimsen Joshi, Kishori Amonkar, Kumar Gandharva, Pandit Jasraj, Ravi Shankar, Vijay Raghav Rao, Hariprasad Chaurasia, Zakir Hussain, Sumitra Guha, Pandit Bhajan Sopori, Shivkumar Sharma, Annapurna Devi, Ali Akbar Khan, and Aashish Khan, Pt. Vishwanath Rao Ringe among other notable performers.

Among the most popular living performers of Carnatic Music are D. K. Pattammal, Dr.M. Balamuralikrishna, Dr. K. J. Yesudas, T V

Sankaranarayanan, Madurai T N Seshagopalan, Aruna Sayeeram, Sudha Ragunathan, Bombay Jayashree and T N Krishnan. M. S. Subbulakshmi was one of the greatest carnatic vocalists ever. M L Vasanthakumari, G N Balasubramaniam, Dr. S. Ramanathan, Chembai Vaidyanatha Bhagavatar, Vidwan Gopala Pillai is famous musical legends who lived in the last century.

CHAPTER – 2

Indian music as

"THE THERAPEUTIC HEALER"

- Nada Yoga.
- Nadopasna
- Chanting and toning.
- Raga Chikitsa.
- Tala, Rhythm and the Heartbeats.
- *The primacy of the voice and the association of the musical sound with prayer.*
- The healing power of 'AUM'

CHAPTER 2
INDIAN MUSIC AS "THE THERAPEUTIC HEALER"

This is discovered in ancient India that there are seven basic musical notes, which were derived from sounds of nature. Through meditation, we can feel that each note corresponds to a certain chakra, or energy wheel, within us. The chakra becomes activated when the frequency of the note matches that of the corresponding chakra and can be strengthened by it. By using the notes in certain combinations, the connection between the chakras is also activated. In such a way, the beauty of music has the power to heal mind, body and soul. Music is often considered the medicine of the mind. This universal language of the mankind not only bridges borders made by human beings, but also has a profound effect on human psyche and body. The power of music that can cure the heart and mind is now being used in certain healing therapies as well. This had led to the birth of the term 'Music Therapy'.

The interpersonal process in which music and all its facets are used by the therapists, to help their patients in improving or maintaining their health, is termed "Music Therapy".

As we all know that Music is an inseparable part of our lives and knowingly or unknowingly it has certain effects on all of us. Let us explore the depth of historical grounds of Indian music in context of music practices and music therapy.

Nada Yoga

As we all know, that there are two types of the musical sound called 'Nada' and they are named as- 'Aahata Nada' and 'Anahata Nada'. And in context to Indian Music and Music Therapy, we will talk about both of them.

Nada Yoga has its roots in the Vedas. It is the science of Divine vibration, as revealed to the Mystics, Saints and Yogis who have used it to reach Self-Realization, the experience of Oneness with Brahman, the Supreme Consciousness. Nada Yoga involves a tuning into subtler vibrations, one's internal music and sounds, until ultimately one reaches a state where there is absolute silence and peace, returning to the source of creation, to God. This state is attainable by an individual who has reached a high level of purification through his Sadhana.

Although many have attempted to dissect and analyze Nada Yoga, it is not just an intellectual pursuit but rather an experiential one. That is why the Nada Yogi delves into the practice without having to fully understand it, striving for the state that will lead to complete absorption and experience.

The vehicle for its transmission is Indian classical music in the form of Ragas, Talas, Slokas, Mantras, chanting, Kirtan and Bhajans. One does not have to be an established Nada Yogi or learned in Vedanta philosophy to practice. Anyone can be involved in this, whether educated or uneducated, as long as they chant the name of God with love and devotion. This practice will help to purify the body, mind, emotions and intellect, creating transformation so that one can tune into the subtler internal vibrations.

The aim of all Yoga paths is to refine the whole personality so that the light of the Divine Self shines through in all of splendour. Ultimately every form of Yoga, whether it is Hatha Yoga, Raja Yoga, Karma Yoga, Bhakti

Yoga, Jnana Yoga, Nada Yoga etc., if practiced earnestly and with unwavering discipline, will culminate in Nada Yoga, the experience of the Anahata Nada. The different paths of Yoga are designed to suit different personalities.

While the best Yoga practice is one that integrates the various paths, such as Sampoorna Yoga, someone with a natural sense of music will obviously have a proclivity to place more emphasis on the aspect of Nada Yoga. But it is not just for the musically inclined. Nada Yoga uses Divine music to move from the gross differentiated vibrations to the subtlest state until it reaches the source. It enchants and stills the mind so that it becomes completely absorbed in Divine vibration, which is the essence underlying all of creation.

According to the Vedas, Brahman, the One without a second, manifests as this universe in the form of vibration, which modern scientists refer to as the big bang. The first manifestation of the Absolute is referred to as "Om," Pranava or Nada Brahman. This is the Para state, which is the most subtle undifferentiated vibration, the immutable essence underlying all of creation. While this concept is elusive and difficult to grasp with our limited intellect, Vedanta and Samkhya philosophy provide some insight.

When the creative aspect of Brahman becomes many, its energy aspect, Prakriti (the term used in Vedanta and Samkhya philosophy) or Shakti (the term used in Tantric tradition) manifests as this universe. Prakriti or Shakti is nature, the Divine Mother, and descends into this creation from the most subtle to the gross. From the Para state, this primordial energy interacting with Purusha, which is pure consciousness, becomes more differentiated and manifests into the three Gunas, which are the three inseparable forces expressed in all of creation. They are: Sattwa, a state of balance; Rajas, a state of activity and movement; and Tamas a state of inertia or darkness. This level of manifestation is still subtle and is referred to as the Pashyanti state. The three Gunas, in their subtle state, are in the transcendental realm, which is beyond the ability of mind and intellect to grasp. Therefore, one can only experience it in the transcendental state through meditation. As these Gunas begin to combine with one another, the state of mental vibration, known as the Madhyama state, is created. Here, one can relate to the vibration in the form of universal concepts. For example, when you think of water, regardless of what your language, culture, or geographical location, the mental concept of water, the liquid that quenches your thirst, will still be the same. No matter how you express it in words or sounds, the concept is still the same. The last state is the Vaikhari state, in which this world of objects, names and forms, sound, language and music can be perceived through the senses, which of course, are interpreted by the mind.

Since every aspect of our being is greatly influenced by sound vibration, the ancient Masters formulated the system of Nada Yoga, starting with the audible level (Vaikhari state) to which we can most easily relate, for purification and Self- Realization. Nada Yoga is a very practical science because it addresses our very essence.

Nada Yoga refines and attunes all the bodily systems, the Nadis (the subtle channels through which energy flows), the mind and the intellect through sound vibration using external instruments such as the Veena, the Sarangi, the Sitar, the Guitar, the Sarod, the Harmonium or the Tabla. The body and the voice are the greatest instruments. One may study and learn the technical notes, Talas and Ragas, but it is for the sole purpose of transformation and Self-Realization. While singing or playing an instrument, one develops focus, concentration and absorption. Once the bodily equipment (physical, pranic, mental, intelletual and egoic systems) is refined and purified and the mind gradually becomes internalized, one is taken to higher levels of awareness and consciousness until ultimately, the individual consciousness realizes its Oneness with the Supreme Consciousness and the goal of Yoga is reached. As the mind becomes still and internalized, one experiences the Nadam, vibration, including the subtle movement of Prana and the Anahata sound, one's internal music, which is a mean to take you to the state of Samadhi. At that stage, the external instrument becomes redundant. This refinement and purification of the personality is a step-by-step process and takes many years of dedicated practice to reach that advanced state.

Thus, one should pursue the path of transformation, continuing the disciplines of purification and refinement through Nada Yoga, so that one may eventually experience the Anahata sound. Now the question which comes on mind is **"What is the Anahata sound?"** It is something distinct and different from the Ahata Nada. Ahata Nada is sound vibration that is experienced on the sensual level. For example, if someone strikes a drum, that vibration will travel through the air into the hearing mechanism in your body and you will hear the drum beat. The Anahata Nada, however, is experienced in the state of meditation as the subtle vibrations of Prana. With the mind internalized, one can hear an unstuck sound. In other words, the experience of the Anahata Nada does not require an external instrument to hear it.

There are different levels of infoldment in the experience of Anahata Nada. Successively, one will hear chinnechinne, the sound of the ocean, the kunch, the kettledrums, the drum, the lute, the flute, the harp and the clapping of thunder. In the practice of Hatha Yoga, as the Granthis are pierced, different sounds or vibrations are experienced, as explained in subsequent Slokas. But do not stop there because they are not the ultimate goal. They are just stages that are reached in one's spiritual development. Every successive level is a sign that one is delving deeper and deeper within. The sounds charm the mind to dive into deeper levels of consciousness until one is able to pierce through the last veil and experience the Self without any conditioning.

"Gunghat ke pat khol re tohe piya milenge"

The reason why Indian classical music is the vehicle for the practice of Nada Yoga is because it has been perfected already. It was not developed but instead flowed through the minds of purified beings. It is the knowledge of the universe, knowledge of the Vedas. Veda literally means pure and perfect knowledge. The knowledge about Nada Yoga, which is contained in the Sama Veda, has been handed down from Guru to disciple as a systematic science. Since this knowledge is already perfect, nothing can be added to it.

When music is practiced to transform the personality with a view of becoming more refined and humble, then, such an implementation of music is called 'Nada Yoga'. The ancient system of Nada Yoga, which dates back to the time of Tantras, has fully acknowledged the impact of music on body and mind and put into practice the vibrations emanating from sounds to uplift one's level of consciousness.[1]

Nadopasana

Nadopasana is bhakti, worship, and devotion through music. As the article on Thyagaraja's musical plays pointed out, Sri Thyagaraja Swami used his compositions to energize our inner spiritual forces or nadopasana to attain moksha or salvation in this life. There are several references to nadopasana in Indian musicology, philosophy, and epics. For example, in The Sangita-Rathnakara, the opening slokas explain how nada and Kundalini are inter-related and how this comprehension is necessary for salvation. Sri Thyagaraja Swami took the first three slokas and composed the following kritis, Nada Thanum Anisam, Sobhillu Saptha Swara, and Nadopasana, using the first, second, and third sloka respectively.

According to Hindu shastras, Naabhi, Hrith, Kanta, Rasana, and Naasa are the sources of sound which originate from the Mooladhara or the inner soul. The recognition of this Mooladharanaada is itself moksha says Sri Thyagaraja in the Sankarabharanamkriti, Swara Raga Sudharasa. In this connection, it is interesting to note that Sir John Sparrow, in his book titled, Serpent Power, equates Kundalini with endogenous sound. The identification of the correct shrutis as the home of the swaras is also important for experiencing moksha or liberation "Saptha Swarmula Grhuhamulaguruthemokshamura." The worship of pure sound emanating from within you and identifying yourself with it and being in consonance with it is liberation or moksha.

Sri Thyagaraja Swami not only stresses the importance of recognizing and developing the ability to experience Mooladhara nada, but also more specifically asks the votaries to practice sangitopasana as a mean and prelude to enjoy nadopasana. In his composition, Sribapriya

Sangeethopasana in Atana, he conjures up visions of the mind travelling in the swaras - "Sapthaswara Chaari" and melodic ragas manifesting themselves in delightful forms –

"Ranjimpacheseduragambulu, manjulamagunavatarambulethi."

He stresses other and nearer terrestrial benefits of sangita gana–

"Prema Bhakthi, Sujana Vathsalyamu, Srimath Ramaavara Katakshamu, Nema Nishta Yasodhanamu" as the rewards of acquiring Sangita Sastragnana.

These discussions on nadopasana thus point out how Sri Thyagaraja was not only an excellent musicologist conforming to the traditional sastras but who, through simple songs with pristine purity, taught us the nature and purpose of music. Indeed, through sangita he urged us to acquire the wisdom of perceiving Brahman, the intelligence to analyze and experience Him; the diligence to seek Him; and the patience to wait for enlightenment. *"He described his Rama as an embodiment of Nada. No other composer has in such a simple and appealing ways taught music as art, science, philosophy and ultimately, as a mean to salvation."*

The higher form of meditation is therefore considered to bemeditation on the principal of sound (nada) which is symbolized by the sacred syllable AUM, a syllable said to include all the possibilities of speech since it is made of a guttural, a labial and a nasal sound, all other sounds being unavoidably contained within this triangle.[1]

According to Yoga shastras, we humans are a microcosmic image of the universe. This universal energy that each human carries within oneself is

---

the Kundalini. The Kundalini lies dormant until awakened. The object of certain forms of yoga is to awaken this dormant force and to let it lead us to the path of salvation. Liberation, therefore, is unity with the universe from which we originated; the individual spirit becomes part of the universal spirit. It is the highest experience that a yogi to a saint to an ordinary individual is striving to reach. One of the yogic approaches that awaken the Kundalini is the nada or nadopasana or devotion through music.

Chanting and Toning

Music has remained an integral part of the Indian culture since antiquity. Musical instruments like the sarod, sarangi, tabla and sitar which are very popular in the world of music today had also been a part of the ancient Indian music. Gazals, khayal, tala, gharana and raga are the musical genres of the Indian classical music. In ancient India, music used to be a part of the famous Sanskrit dramas like Mircha-katika and Abhijnana-Shakuntalam. The origin of the ancient Indian music began in the age of the Aryans, with the chanting of the Vedas.

As earlier said, chanting of the Vedas in Aryan age brought the concept of music in ancient Indian culture. The hymns chanted by the priests in the temples followed a musical tone. The priests also pronounced the Sanskrit vocalizing syllables in their chants. These were called Sthobhaksharas. The music was finally created with the rhythm and melody. References of the ancient Indian music can be found in the Vedas, Puranas, Upanishads, epics and Srimad Bhagavata Gita.[1]

Indian music and mantras bring us back into the physical world every day. This used to be a tradition in ancient times with kings and saints.

Most of the early Indian music was written by saints for devotion and meditation. The kings, like the people, wanted to live in peace amidst all the problems of administration. So, they employed the musicians to create Indian music for the different times of day to give them better feelings.

The Vedic period religions laid the foundation of the religious practices that are continued till date in modern India. These religions arose from the sacred scriptures that were composed during the Vedic period. These scriptures founded the very base of Hinduism in India. The scriptures that talk of the various religious practices are basically the four Vedas namely Rig Veda, Yajur-Veda, Sama-Veda and Atharva-Veda. The Upanishads are also considered to be a part of the Vedas and contain valuable information regarding the rituals and religions of Vedic Age.[1]

The principles of religions in Vedic Era were basically laid down by the priests, who were the highest class of people in the society. They were the ones who performed the rituals, chanted hymns and read out holy texts in temples and functions. The texts recorded in the Vedas were supposed to have divine power and were to be chanted perfectly with the right tone, pronunciation and emphasis. This was believed to make the hymns effective to the hilt and gain the maximum power out of it.[2]

Religion in early Vedic period revolved around crude forms of worshipping which basically includes nature worship. This means that people in the early Vedic period worshipped different forms of nature as god like sun, earth, moon, wind, rain, fire and other natural phenomena. Since there were no scientific explanations for natural phenomena like rain, thunder, wind, etc. people feared them and thus worshipped them. Chanting of prayers and hymns were a common practice to invoke the Gods.

The later Vedic age saw the increase in powers of the priests and they formed the highest class in the society. Religious practices were refined and worship of Gods in the form of idols gained importance. Animal sacrifice also increased during this period. With rituals and hymns taking centre stage, the evolution of Hindu religion took place. Nature worship gave rise to new beliefs and new Gods. The duty of imparting the religious know how to people was the duty of the priests.

Chanting of the Suktas was famous in ancient times and they still are in vogue. And some of the suktas are even now being performed as they have the connectivity with body, mind and soul. Such as, Agni-Sukta is a prayer paid to god fire and also Swasti-Vachan is a prayer sukta paid to god. Chanting creates the vibrations in the environment which lead to a particular impact and music gives it a particular effect and base. Also, in Vedic times music was developed with its all seven notes. And these suktas used to be performed musically in so many rituals and ceremonies.

When we are discussing the power of Sound in context of Music, then first of all we must know that how do we acquire the use of music as a language for expression and communication? To the younger version of our selves, language is music. A new born hears a symphony of diverse abstract sounds; language has not yet become representational. "The infant lacks the capacity of relating to language as a semantic system, to its symbols and concepts, he is responding to the various sound components – intensity, pitch, rhythm and timbre...If we could turn back and identify with the infant, hearing the wood around us through infantile ears, might not be the secrets of music unveil themselves before us, enabling us to understand its paths of expression?"[1]

The infant cannot comprehend specific meaning in verbal communication, but the "inarticulate, preverbal music of mood and intent is a constant undercurrent in speech"[2]. Words are nothing more than sounds arranged in patterns, and yet the infant recognizes the essential import of these patterns, and that the patterns have significance. This attachment of significance to sound patterns precedes actual comprehension. It is the repetition of sound patterns which reinforce the pattern's particular significance. The very act of repetition serves as a link between the parent and child, a notice of regularity.

This early mode of expression and communication between parent and child creates within us the latent ability to utilize sounds as meaningful expression. Just as the parent assists the newborn, the music therapist helps the new client to feel comfortable using the elements of music for expression and communication.

Sound in relation to music reveals a truth. This is discovered in ancient India that there are seven basic musical notes, which were derived from sounds of nature or songs of various animals. Through meditation, we can feel that each note corresponds to a certain chakra, or energy wheel, within us. The chakra becomes activated when the frequency of the note matches that of the corresponding chakra and can be strengthened by it. By using the notes in certain combinations, the connection between the chakras is also activated.

In Indian music SA – the root note- corresponds to the Mooladhara, the chakra at the base of the spine. This is the protector of the subtle system and therefore SA is present in all the scales and is constant. Four notes in the Indian scale can be sharpened, or lowered – RE (2nd), GA (3rd), DHA (6th), NI (7th). One note can be sharpened, or raised – MA (4th). PA (5th) is also a constant like SA. By using mantras, or affirmations, we not only invoke the qualities of the chakras with the name of the deity present at that chakra, but we can also use the notes that give the strongest effect.[1]

In our day-to-day life, we find that all the seven chakras are not active all the time. Some do not work properly, as there are some hindrances, due to lack of required energy power. Since these chakras are connected with different organs, any hindrance in their functioning creates physical imbalance in the person. Emotional and mental imbalances are also seen depending upon the state of the chakras.[2]

While discussing Toning we again will have to check the past records of the Vedic times.

_____

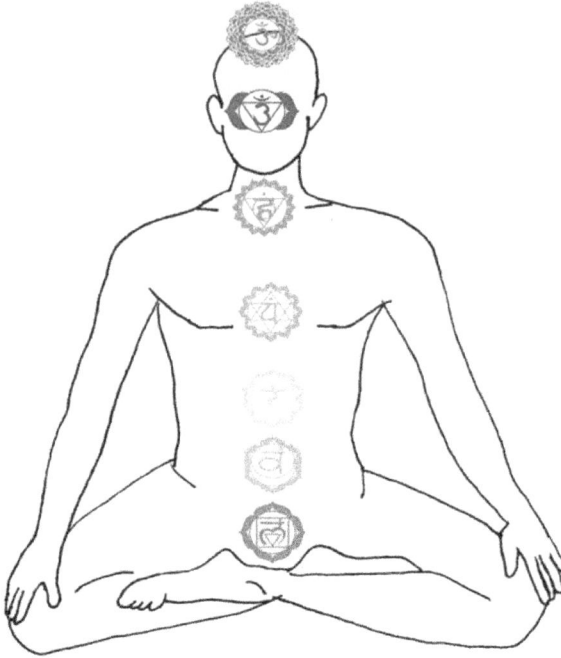

Raga Chikitsa

Definite form of ragas emerged during the classical-cum-epic period. Before the Ramayana was compiled in a book form (400 B.C.), seven pure (shuddha) jatis (jatiragas) evolved in the beginning of the classical period (600-500 B.C.). In Ramayana we find the use of seven shuddhajatis or jatiragas in songs. The jatis were the casual or basic ragas, from which evolved all kinds of ragas, marga and desi. The term jati connotes the idea of the universal (samanya) like the Brahmana, kshatriya castes, etc. It is like the main die wherein all the ragas were casted alike. It is therefore regarded as the main source or fountainhead of all the melodic forms.[1]

Raga, we all know is the sequence of selected notes (swaras) that lend appropriate `mood' or emotion in a selective combination. Depending on their nature, a raga could induce or intensify joy or sorrow, violence or peace and it is this quality which forms the basis for musical application. Thus, a whole range of emotions and their nuances could be captured and communicated within certain rhythms and melodies. Playing, performing and even listening to appropriate ragas can work as a medicine. Various ragas have since been recognized to have definite impact on certain ailments.[2]

Simply defined, *Raga Chikitsa* means "healing through the use of raga."Raga-Ragini Vidya is defined as "the knowledge of how to use raga for the purposes of healing. The method of healing through music is a lost ancient art and that is being revived in modern times. Identification of the Indian Classical Ragas (Carnatic) and their consonance with the elements of nature (panchabhutas) help in tracing the concepts related to "Music for Healing and Meditation. The way of rendering music and treatment of raga is generalised not outside the frame of orthodox tradition. Music is considered as the fourth Upaveda, the Ganclharva Veda, in addition to Dhanarveda, Ayurveda, and ArthaShastra. The devotional music acts as the means of spiritual energy transmission. Some Higher Force takes care of this process, when it is once decided to heal through music. Swara Shuddhi (pure notes) is held in great veneration and is considered as a standard of musical truth. Melody (raga) is the result of Swara Shuddhi. There is clarity and pure energy in such a melody."[1] One of the unique and fundamental features of Raga-Ragini Vidya is the classification of the ragas based on their elemental composition (weather, air, fire, water, earth) and the proper use of the elements to balance the nature of the imbalance. This is the basic healing methodology of Ayurveda, as well. Another unique and fundamental aspect of this method is the Vedic recognition that each of the seven swara (notes) has a presiding deity and that the qualities of the deities and their relation hips to the raga as an entity is of paramount importance for the proper use of the raga as a healing modality.[2]

The ancient Hindus had relied on music for its curative role: the chanting and toning involved in Veda mantras in praise of God have been used from time immemorial as a cure for several disharmonies in the individual as well as his environment. Several sects of `bhakti' such as Chaitanya sampradaya, Vallabha sampradaya have all accorded priority to music. Historical records, too, indicate that one. Haridas Swami who was the guru of the famous sixteenth-century musician Tan Sen in Emperor Akbar's (1542-1605 AD) time, is credited with the recovery of illness of one of the queens of the Emperor with a selected raga.

The great composers of classical music in India called the `Musical Trinity', - who were curiously the contemporaries of the `Trinity of Western Classical Music, Bach, Beethoven and Mozart- were quite sensitive to the acoustical energies. Legend has it that Saint Thyagaraja brought a dead person back to life with his Bilahari composition Naa Jiva Dhaara. Muthuswamy Dikshitar's Navagriha Kriti is believed to cure stomach ache. Shyama Sastry's composition Duru Sugu uses music to pray for good health.[1]

Raga chikitsa was an ancient manuscript, which dealt with the therapeutic effects of raga. The library at Thanjavur is reported to contain such a treasure on ragas that spells out the application and use of various ragas in fighting common ailments.[2]

Living systems show sensitivity to specific radiant energies - be it acoustical, magnetic or electro-magnetic. As the impact of music could be easily gauged on emotions and thereby on mind, it can be used as a tool believed to control the physiological, psychological and even social activities of the patients.

Indian classical music can be classified into two forms: kalpita-sangita or composition, which is previously conceived, memorized, practised and rendered and manodharma-sangita or the music extemporised and performed. The latter can be equated to the honey-mooner's first night as it conceives both spontaneity and improvisation. It is fresh and natural as it is created almost on the spot and rendered instantly on the spur of the moment.

According to an ancient Indian text, Swara-Shastra, the seventy-two melakarta ragas (parent ragas) control the 72,000 important nadis or nerves in the body, which are believed to transmit life energy into every cell of the body. It is believed that if one sings with due devotion, adhering to the raga lakshana (norms) and sruti-shuddhi, (pitch purity) the raga could affect the particular nerve in the body in a favourable manner.[1]

While the descending notes in a raga (avarohana) do create inward-oriented feelings, the ascending notes (arohana) represent an upward mobility. Thus music played for the soldiers or for the dancers has to be more lively and uplifting with frequent use of arohana content. In the same way, melancholic songs should go for `depressing' avarohanas. Although it is not a rule, most of the Western tunes based on major keys play joyful notes, while those composed in minor keys tend to be melancholic or serious.

Certain ragas do have a tendency to move the listeners, both emotionally as well as physically. An involuntary nod of the head, limbs or body could synchronize with lifting tunes when played.

Music can however be an essential instrument in the meditation process, and indeed its main factor. At this point, it is music itself that becomes the subject of meditation. But not all kinds of music are suitable for this purpose. Structures of correlated sounds through which the mind can wander- we could say "improvisations" like the Indian ragas, can be and are in fact a remarkable instrument for mental concentration.

The process of music created through the raga is nothing more than an exteriorized form of meditation.[1]

Here it is necessary to mention an incident which took place in the court of great emperor of India 'Akbar': Once, Akbar asked his court's best singer and the renowned music maestro Tansen, to sing "Deepak" raga. Tansen tried his best not to sing it because it could create havoc in the court, but Akbar wanted to see that havoc himself. Tansen sang the Deepak Raga. First the courtier started feeling warmth, then gradually they saw that all the lamps had lighted, then they started burning and they saw that the curtains of the court has started burning. The fire had set. Everybody got worried. What to do now. Tansen's daughter also sang very well. Somebody suggested to call her, andcool-down the court. She was called and she immediately started singing "Megh-Malhar" Raga. Surprisingly, after a while it started raining, gradually the warmth decreased, and fire was put out. He is also credited for creating raga Darbari-Kanhada.[2]

Some ragas like Darbari-Kanhada, Kamaj and Pooriya are said to help in defusing mental tension, particularly in the case of hysterics. For those who suffer from hypertension, ragas such as Ahir-Bhairav, Pooriya and Todi are prescribed. To control anger and bring down the violence within, Carnatic ragas like Punnagavarali, Sahana etc. do come handy. It is generally believed in music circles, though scientific endorsement doesn't appear to be forthcoming.

Sh. T. V. Sairam experimenting on the impact of raga on mentally-retarded (MR) children has noticed that it is the right combination of rhythms and tempo, which also affect the quality of a raga.[1]

Not only psychological impact, but also somatic or physiological impact of ragas has come to light in some recent works. (Sairam, 2004b). For instance, digestion is reported to be activated with Hindustani ragas such as Deepak which is believed to cure acidity. For constipation, the musical folk remedy is Gunkali or Jaunpuri. Malkauns or Hindolam are said to control fevers. Fevers like malaria are also said to be controlled by the ragas like Marva. For headaches, relaxing with the ragas like Durbari-Kanada, Jayjaywanti and Sohni are said to be beneficial. The Chennai-based tiny Nada Centre for Music Therapy has quite recently embarked on raga therapy research to re-discover the therapeutic ragas by trial and error methods and some modest progress is already visible giving green signals. There is a growing awareness that ragas could be a safe alternative for many medical interventions.

Simple interactive musical rhythms with low pitched swaras, as in bhajans and kirtans are the time-tested sedative, which can even substitute the synthetic analgesics, which show many a side-effects. They are capable of leading to relaxation, as observed with the alpha-levels of the brain waves. They may also lead to favourable hormonal changes in the system.It is therefore felt that there is an urgent need for further detailed enquiry to be based on scientific parameters, which will go a long way in unearthing the goldmine on which the Indian musical system is resting now.

Tala, Rhythm and the Heartbeats

In the Natya-sastra, Bharata has said:

$$\text{"कालस्यत्प्रप्राप्रंवप्रविज्ञप्रयंताला-योक्त्रिभि:"}$$

Really the existence of time (kaal) is easily perceived with the help of rhythm (taal) and vice-versa. The term 'tempo' is known as laya as well as mana, and the term 'rhythm' as taal or paat. The 'Laya' is but the intervening time or space between two units of time or kaal. So, laya is conceived as evolved from kaal or taal.

Bharata has also said:

$$\text{"काल-कला-प्रप्राप्रप्रनटलितयभिधीयतप्र"}$$

i.e. the term 'taal' conveys the idea of the combination of kaal and kala.[1]

Tal, (variously transliterated as *"tala", "taal"* or *"taala"*) is the Indian system of rhythm. It has been argued that rhythm is fundamental to the creation of any musical system. Certainly from a historic standpoint, rhythm existed many centuries before the word *rag* was ever used. Given

---

.

this historical pre-eminence, it is not surprising that rhythm occupies an important position in the Indian system of music.

The word *tal*. *Tal* literally means "clap". Today, the *tabla* has replaced the clap in the performance, but the term still reflects the origin. The basic concepts of tal are: tali or bhari, khali, vibhag or (ang), matra , bol, theka, lay, sam and avartan.

Tala in Indian Carnatic Music is a time measure or rhythm cycle. As heart beat is to life for a man, Tala lends life for whole of a concert. It is said **"Sruthi Mata Laya Pita"** which means, the drone emanated from the Tambura is Mother to the music and the Tala is like father. The tala or time in Music is a series of counts made by the wave of hand or tap of the hand on the lap or by using both the hands in a manner of clap.

The very heart-beat of music is Laya. Rhythm is omnipresent. There is rhythm in the movement of heavenly bodies just as in the life cycles of micro-organisms. It is only natural that man is endowed with it. Whenever we listen to music, we look for the rhythmic movements in it and then find ourselves tapping our feet or clapping our hands or even dancing to it. But what exactly do we mean by rhythm? Rhythm can be defined as a process in which the nucleuses of attention are separated by individual parts of time. Whenever we listen to music, we cannot but perceive rhythm. Rhythm gives stability and form to music. It can be described as the tangible gait of any musical movement. In music, this is referred to as Laya. The common fallacy (myth) is that rhythm or laya is confined to percussion instruments and the rhythmic patterns produced therein.

The rhythmic aspects in music are arguably among the most developed and sophisticated across the world. The patterns range from the simple to the complex. The study of rhythmic aspects involves understanding the terms Tala and Laya. Tala is often confused with Laya. Laya refers to the inherent rhythm in anything. Irrespective of whether it is demonstrated or not, it is always present. This can be better illustrated with an example. We know that the sun, the planets and other heavenly bodies are moving objects. Even as our earth rotates on its axis and revolves around the sun, these bodies have their own fixed movements and speeds. Even a microscopic disturbance in that speed may lead to disasters of huge proportions. So laya can be explained as the primordial (ancient) orderliness of movements. Expression of laya in an organised fashion through fixed time cycles is known as Tala. Thus it serves as the structured rhythmic meter to measure musical time-intervals. Tala in music is usually expressed physically by the musician through accented beats and unaccented finger counts or a wave of the hand. In other words, Tala is but a mere scale taken for the sake of convenience.

Mankind has used rhythm healing for centuries, and we still see music being used as 'medicinal' in many indigenous cultures. Human beings and everything that surrounds us is vibrating and pulsing with energy of varying levels of intensity. This energy can pulse at different frequencies and its rhythm can be healing.

It all starts in the womb, as the baby is calmed by a mother's heartbeat. In early childhood it continues with lullabies. This natural pulse or beat generates a good environment for relaxation and reassurance. For many people, the sound of waves on the seashore produces a soothing, relaxing rhythmic pulse, which calms the brain.

When music and its rhythm are fully appreciated it can have a very positive impact upon us. It can, for example-

- Slow down and normalize brain wave patterns

- Stabilize heartbeat, breathing and blood pressure

- Reduce muscle tension, improve body movement and encourage body co-ordination

- Increase the release of endorphins, the body's own pain killers producing that feel good factor

- Boost immune functions

- Help to unwind and relax naturally

- Strengthen memory power and learning capability

- Stimulate the digestive system

- Increases energy levels

It is believed that the music that induces rhythm healing, in practically every culture, has been created using the **heartbeat** as its core.

This healing rhythm is around 60-76 beats per minute. This 'perfect pulse' can be found everywhere in nature in various guises such as waves, rain, rustling leaves, a babbling stream as the water cascades over the stones, the crackle of an open fire, and the breathing of a sleeping child.

The primacy of the voice and the association of the musical sound with prayer

The primacy of the voice and the association of the musical sound with prayer have their very routes in the history of Indian Music.

Well has it been said by Amulya Charan Vidyabhushan:

"It was incumbent on all at that period (Vedic), to conduct their sacrifices strictly according to the Vedic rites, and music played an important part in the ceremonies. In the conduct the Ashvamedha-yajna (horse sacrifice), two veena players were required to play their instruments. One of these was to be a Brahmin, who would play by day, and the other a Kshatriya, who performed at night.[1]

As we all know that Indian music has enriched our culture as well as our souls. But, if we examine the base of our statement then scientifically the sound which is the medium of any musical form is the king and the feel which comes out of that particular sound is the queen. Be it is a love song, an instrumental musical piece or a prayer paid to god. In ancient times, Indian music used to have the mantras, slokas and richas of rigveda which all when used to be sung created the feel of divinity and the better understanding of the importance of the music and the musical sounds. The vocal part of music was fully established by that time. So many prayers were there which were used to be paid to god by the voice and vocals with the sound and the different ways to voice those sounds.

The famous writer Shakespeare once wrote: **"If music be the food of love, play on..."** Profound words, true, but the Bard failed to mention that music is not just nourishment for the heart, but also for the soul. In every culture, music arose from devotional chants and invocations. In India, schools such as yoga and tantra equate **Nada Brahman**, the primordial sound, with the Absolute. The origins of Indian music can be traced back to the chanting of the Sama Veda nearly 4,000 years ago. The primacy of the voice and the association of musical sound with prayer, were thus established early in the history of Indian music.

Though, It is not just the voice or sound which comprises music, it is also the particular feel, melody and the power which music has, to enrich the soul and feed different emotions. It has been a long time when music came into the social existence in India. Ancient musical history of Indian Music proves it well. At first Music was associated with different prayers and thus it is said in context of Indian music **"BRAHMANAND SAHODAR"** which means that music is the almighty. Prayer in any form can heal, protect and keep us calm and when music is almighty then there is no need to explain it any further that Music which has the primacy of voice or sound and has an association with prayer, is the greatest power to heal and maintain the balance in one's life.

The healing power of 'AUM'

Perhaps the most important aspect of sound in the Indian context is the word *'Aum'*—considered the manifested sound of the Divine, and said to hold a powerful influence over the human mind. It is believed that vibrations created by the circular structure of the syllables define the entire cosmos. It is believed to be a truth that if we utter OM consistently and regularly, we send forth signals into the surroundings. We thus demonstrate our intention to serve the plan and our dependability. This attracts the attention of the Higher Ones. The Devas, guiding the activity of the planet know that a worker is available and can be utilised. Not many things are demanded to get into that kind of work,

but to prepare oneself correctly with a spiritual tool. This should act as an incentive to make our outer life coincide with the spiritual impulse.[1]

The Hierarchy uses the holy sound OM to create thought forms. These are sent into areas of crises in order to neutralise tensions. During the last decades humanity went through dangerous times. There were many provocations, which could have led to a serious disaster. We only know the disasters which have happened. The disasters which have been avoided or averted are not known to an average mind. The persons who play key roles on the planet or are in influential positions had a lot of restraint, so that they precipitated only few actions in spite of all provocations. To utter OM regularly in groups has a better effect on the subtle planes for world peace than peace demonstrations.

When planetary crises can be neutralised with the help of OM, it is obvious that also individual crises can well be neutralised. OM removes personality problems and frees us from mental programming. It is also good to consciously connect with OM while falling asleep. Groups can utter OM In order to purify a house, a settlement or a town from unwanted thought forms or to prepare activities for the social welfare. It can be sung in hospitals and healing centres in order to propose alleviation and even to heal the ill. The best and lasting help you can give to a dying person is to gather a group surrounding him and to softly utter OM. This helps with a good departure and a good arrival as well. In the Vedas, it says: When you utter OM, the angels of all seven planes are awakened and the undesirable is expelled. When we collectively utter OM, we build a cone into space which extends and enables the descent of energy into us.[2]

OM can be uttered at all times, preferably in the dawn and dusk hours. We should invoke it in the heart centre or in the brow centre and utter it in a slow, soft, deep and uniform way. It produces a resonance in the whole body that we should observe. If the vibration becomes silent again, we sing the OM anew. The holy word can be uttered three times, five times or in units of seven, i.e. 7, 14, 21, 28 times etc. In this, we can consciously travel with each OM from centre to centre, from above downwards, then from below upwards and back again. We should feel its vibration in the entire body, from the base centre to the head centre and even beyond. In this way, OM helps us to consciously set the energies in motion, and afterwards we feel an alignment of the lower centres to the higher ones. OM should not be uttered mechanically. If so we are like a cassette recorder that doesn't know what it is playing. We would use the throat to utter the sound vocally, but not get the benefit of what we are doing. Also, animals cannot intone the sound, only man can utter and listen. We also have to be careful and responsible with OM: If we don't use fire correctly and burn our fingers in it, it lies not with the fire, but with us. OM is a monosyllabic, a disyllabic and a dissyllabic sound. As the tri-syllabic sound AUM, it represents the trinity: stands for the Father, for the Son and for the Mother. When we contact the pulsating principle of expansion and contraction, we arrive at the bi-syllabic sound of OM. Continuously listening to how this sound happens in us finally leads to hearing the monosyllabic, humming sound. There are several ways for uttering OM. If the emphasis is on A, we are working more with the spirit or with the first ray. If the emphasis is on U, we are working more with the second ray or the soul, representing the balance between spirit and matter. The emphasis on M is good for the manifestation of a work. If we want to manifest acts of good will, we can use OM and thereby emphasise more on the M. If we aim at spiritualising something, we can emphasise the A and the U, giving rise to OM.[1]

"The goal which all the Vedas declare, which all austerities aim at, and which men desire when they lead the life of continence is Om. This syllable Om is indeed Brahman. Whosoever knows this syllable obtains all that he desires. This is the best support; this is the highest support. Whosoever knows this support is adored in the world of Brahma."[2]

CHAPTER – 3

Music Therapy

- *What is Music Therapy?*
- *The constitution of Music Therapy - Beyond the Boundaries.*
- *Role of Music Therapy in healing the Mankind*

CHAPTER 3
MUSIC THERAPY

WHAT IS MUSIC THERAPY

The beauty of music has the power to heal mind, body and soul. Music is often considered the medicine of the mind. This universal language of the mankind not only bridges borders made by human beings, but also has a profound effect on human psyche and body.

Here when we are talking about human psyche and the effects of music on human body then it is essential to mention Bhava & Rasa in an art. Bhava and Rasa are the two most important aspects of any art. Great scholars like Abhinav Gupta, Bharata etc. have brought this out more explicitly:

> "In communicating his meaning through his work of art, the artist creates a beauty that sways the feeling of the audience, inducing in their mind a sort of thrill unworldly in nature. This feeling is called Rasa, which is the aesthetic delight-a rapture experienced by the audience or one who's appreciating an art. The artist's purpose of the art creation is to convey and share a certain meaning through his work and this cannot be complete without evoking the necessary Rasa in the person/audience to whom it is targeted. The main requirement for evoking the Rasa or Aesthetic delight, from the piece of art is Bhava. This is described as the emotional experience. Here the audience is transported to a different level of ethereal/blissful experience otherwise unimaginable."[1]

Now, if we will take a turn to the therapeutic aspect of music then we'll find that music stimulates the nerves of a person very mildly and regulates the flow of blood. It creates a power of concentration in the mind, and spreads an agreeable massive sensation all over the body. The person feels, under the influence of music, disposed to receive impressions from outside. It tills his frame and furrows it, and renders it fertile for the reception and growth of ideas. When, for instance, he hears music while playing cricket, he feels that he has to throw himself, heart and soul into the play; when he attends a religious or social ceremony accompanied with music, he feels that the ceremony has begun and that he should be earnest about it. Music makes light things serious, and invests with a sentiment of reality, even imaginary objects. It spreads a charm over the mind, a slight form of intoxication, under which objects appear as if surrounded with an atmosphere of imagination and fancy. It also gives rise to emotion, and, sustains it for an indefinite length of time.

The way in which music stimulates the mind is peculiar to itself. Some pastimes, as cards, chess, excite the brain and tax its powers to exhaustion. Some games affect particular limbs and bring on muscular disorder, though they contribute to health and vigour within certain limits. The satisfaction of some of the natural desires is agreeable in the beginning, but ends in satiety and even disgust; for an abnormal degree of activity of the nerve and the muscle is then called into play, which necessitates a period of rest soon after. The brain is not put to a strain. The whole body nervous system enters into a state of vibration, which, being uniformed throughout, does not differ much from the normal conditions. There is no loss of energy sustained, but only an equal distribution of it brought about. Its influence begins from the nerve, which it sets in order. Music is, therefore, used as a mean of curing certain nervous diseases - lunacy and other similar affliction which will soon disappear if the diagnosis is correct and well administrated. A musical treat given to the lunatics in an asylum is a great source of comfort to the afflicted, and contributes to the betterment of their condition. Music can relieve pain. Pain is due to an inconvenient vibration of the nerve-cells, caused by some external influence, and music can easily set right such a disorder by means of the regularity of its vibrations. Good music, played during a surgical operation, is a better palliative than the administration of chloroform. In health music creates a mirthful spirit and acts as a good tonic. In sickness, it acts as a medicine. While medicines act from the outside, music proceeds from within. Medicines may go wrong and produce evil effects, but music does no harm, even if it doesn't succeed. Music is, therefore, said to be a healthy and innocent pastime- always pleasing and never tiresome.[1]

It is not generally realized that the actual, ultimate impact of music, be it vocal or instrumental, is inseparable not only from the uniquely trained sensibility and imagination of the rasika, but even from his/her general sense of values. There is, however, yet another relation to which music is necessarily a subject, but which has rarely been made an object of study. This is the relation of music to silence. [2]

Yet, on the other hand, music cannot be said to be real like a thing or an everyday happening. We do not use music as we use tables and chairs. And, where we do employ music for a practical purpose, as in the case of

---

music therapy, we do not really attend to music as art; we rather look upon it as a kind of medical treatment.[1]

The power of music that can cure the heart and mind is now being used in certain healing therapies as well. This had led to the birth of the term 'Music Therapy'. The interpersonal process in which music and all its facets are used by the therapists, to help their patients in improving or maintaining their health, is termed Music Therapy.

Music Therapy is a branch of psychology wherein its mental, physical, emotional, social, aesthetic and spiritual, all the aspects are, individually or combined, to address people's needs. The needs of the client or the patient can be addressed either through the direct use of music or through the relationships that develop between the client and the therapist. Music therapy can be used with individuals of all ages, to help the body fight various diseases and conditions. Music therapy is considered as one of the expressive therapies which entails the use of creative arts as a form of therapy.[2]

Turco-Persian psychologist and music theorist Al-Farabi discussed the therapeutic effects of music on the soul, as early as, the 9th century in his treatise "Meanings of the Intellect". The usage of music to heal is gradually gaining momentum and becoming a growing field of health care.

Music has been known to be in close connection to emotions as well as evoking emotions. Furthermore, researchers have found out that music listeners commonly utilize music for emotion regulation. Because majority

---

of psychiatric disorders are emotional, or caused emotional disorders, it is no wonder that music has been found to be a powerful therapeutic agent. Emotions, images, associations and memories evoked by music offer a valuable view to one's mental processes thus reaching the experiences and qualities that are difficult to deal with, or reach verbally.[1]

On the other hand, experiences with emotional loadings and interaction in general become possible in music therapy even when the verbal expression is not possible. This can be the case with children (even infants), clients with severe developmental disorders, people with dementia, or clients suffering from severe psychiatric disorders such as acute psychosis.

To have a clear idea about Music Therapy, the link between bodily gestures and musical recitation should be strong enough and adequately understood, and, for the same Dr. Ashok D. Ranade in his book "On Music and Musicians of Hindoostan", mentions: *"The intrinsic relationship between gestures and musical expression should be properly understood. Both are inevitably connected for two reasons. Firstly, because singing is, to all purposes, a deliberate deviation from the sound patterns used in day-to-day speech. However deviated speech-patterns hardly prove adequate in themselves unless they are combined with the corresponding gesture-patterns."*

On the other hand, it should be remembered that gesture-patterns are also results of efforts- the coordinated and willed body-responses. Further, gestures also discharge the function of relieving psycho-physiological tensions created by the efforts involved. This is the second reason why gestures are bound to accompany singing- an activity which makes extra demands on the psycho-physical resources normally at one's command as a cumulative result of the two requirements of having matching patterns and tension reliefs.[1]

It has been stated and mentioned in so many research works or books that there were certain bodily gestures at the time of reciting sama gana and it was believed that those body movements have their own connections with chakras to have positive effects on one's mind and life. The way, when a performer is singing or playing a musical instrument, he is making some bodily indications. Those gestures are transmitted to the listeners and different listeners after hearing the played or sung pieces, praise the performer with different body movements. In the same manner when music is used for the therapeutic purpose and the therapist applies the music on the listener, listener starts giving his feedback, first with body movements and after that the stimulations of music changes his mental frame and the listener reciprocates to its results with his better health, mentally and physically, both ways.

In addition to its mind related qualities, music, in particular playing, is active bodily functioning as well. Bodily coordination and motor functioning are often in the focus of music therapy with the clients with motor disabilities. In music therapy with children and adolescents bodily and action based functioning plays often an important role even if the primary emphasis of the therapy is on mental problems.[2]

When using receptive techniques, the rule of thumb that the patient's preferred music usually works best. For instance, in the Finnish stroke study I briefly mentioned in my writing, only patients' preferred music was

---

used. Researchers had to interview the patients, their relatives, and so on, in order to ensure that the music that they used really had a specific meaning to the client. The same piece of music can mean many different things to many different people, and thus, whatever music is used for therapeutic purposes needs to express a particular relationship between the client and the music. For some clients Mozart maybe the right choice, some prefer the Beatles, and so on. Music therapists are usually interested in the experiences (images, memories, etc.) that the patient associates with the music. The tendency is to find the most moving, personal, touching and important music as possible from the client's perspective.

Clinicians know that a piece of music from one's childhood can evoke incredibly strong memories or feelings:

> "This is the music that I used to listen to when I was very sad and I was again sitting in my room feeling loneliness and anger...I clearly remember the atmosphere then and whenever I listen to that song again I feel the same way..."

In this example, music helps the client to really reach the emotional memories from his/her childhood, which was traumatic and that now is under investigation in therapy.[1]

As you can see, it is often not only the music but the relationship between the patient and the therapist, which makes the therapy work. Music can be therapeutic as such on its own, but music therapists have specific techniques at their disposal that they can utilize to access the client's musical experiences in goal-orientated, therapeutic way.

Music is something that you have to concentrate on in a specific way for it to really touch you. Most often in our everyday life music comes and goes; it is everywhere, people don't really attach to it. At the same time, many of us are incredibly selective when it comes to music as well. When a radio station starts playing music that we don't like, we quickly switch to another station.[1] Most often people are unconsciously seeking pleasurable music, music that enforces their mood, solace and so on. But there is also research evidence that some people listen to sad music in order to - probably unconsciously - meet their own sadness (maybe their personal losses, etc.) and deal with it. In this way music facilitates the person going through difficult things in their life.

Most people probably have the bulk of their personal musical experiences listening to his/her favourite music alone and really concentrating on it. In brief, the music that we hear on the radio when we are focusing on something else seldom causes a negative effect because normal/healthy people have also normal and rather strong mental filters and defence mechanisms in use, in their everyday life.

Of course, there are a lot of examples where music has been purposefully used as stimulator, or amplifier of a certain mood - in other words, the desired mood is already there but music is used to boost that mood. For instance, some school shooters are known to have boosted their killing mood by listening to certain music before the event.

During the recent massacre in Norway where 76 young people were killed, the shooter is said to have been wearing earphones and listening to music while doing this unbelievably brutal and merciless thing.[2]

———————————

Music therapy can be applied to various diagnostic groups. Music therapy can be divided to two main categories:

Receptive: music listening based and **Active**: music making. The latter refers to musical self-expression and interaction that often is spontaneous, free improvisation with instruments or voice.[1] Contrary to common conception, music therapy does not presuppose musical skills or talent. In many countries, music therapy is most often applied to children and adolescents, and with people with developmental disorders. According to clinical experience and research, music therapy seems to be a relevant form of treatment also in the field of traditional psychotherapy – for instance in the treatment of adults' mental disorders.

The constitution of Music Therapy - Beyond the Boundaries

According to Claude Levistrauss: "If you know the consciousness of a musician, you know everything in the universe."[2]

Boundaries! The word itself talks about different dimensions and directions. But, when we talk about boundaries in context of music, then this world loses its basic and general meaning and gets completed with the use of another term which is 'Beyond'. Under the heading of **'The constitution of Music therapy beyond the boundaries'** we actually are going to examine the different styles of implementing the same melodious music which has no limitations, no cultural barriers and no discrimination when it comes to the healing process.

As, Mr. Claude Levistrauss has already mentioned, that, to know everything in universe, one just has to reach the consciousness of a

---

musician. Based on this statement we can say that to reach the level of enlightenment we have to be deeply connected to a musician who stands there on the firm base of his music. So, ultimately the musician, from which so ever direction he comes has the music, and if that music is in its pure form, which can stimulate our minds, then the benefits accumulated by that music will also be pure.

The American Pianist, Singer-Songwriter and Composer Mr. Billy Joel said: **"I think music in itself is healing. It's an explosive expression of humanity. It's something we are all touched by. No matter what culture we're from, everyone loves music."**[1]

When music is beyond the boundaries then how can we imagine that the therapeutic role of music should be restricted to only a handful of nations or countries?

Yes! It stands out of the classifications even if it has different ways of implementation when it comes to the clinical music therapy treatment.

Role of Music Therapy in healing the Mankind

Dr. Suvarna Nalapat in her book 'Ragacikitsa (Music Therapy)' quotes: "Communication in Sanskrit is Samvedana, vedana is pain. Music takes away the pains through samvedana and is an aesthetic, but it is the most aesthetic of arts. It communicates at a transcendental level and super conscious states of aesthetics which we call the 'layayogam' or 'nadalayayogam'. The pun of samvedana/vedana and aesthetics/ anaesthetics is interesting. For this to happen at least two people are needed, one is a singer and the other is a listener (in music), one

---

bhagavan and one bhakta (in bhakti sampradaya), one man and one woman (Radhakrisna, sivshakti). Veda calls this a 'Mithuna'. It counld be a guru and sisya or a parent and child or any two people who love each other. Language and music have to convey an idea, a message, an experience or an emotion. They have to touch a listener/ several listeners/readers to attain the fruits of research"[1]

On the basis of the above quote by Dr. Nalapat, this is quite evident that for music therapy we need two persons for the course and this is also to be taken under the consideration that music has a goal to stimulate listeners mind, heart and soul for the fruitful effects on the mental, spiritual and even on the physical state.

Musical experiences which human beings experience are called 'MLP' (musical life panorama).[2] Now in context to music therapy it is essential to know the meaning of the term 'MLP' and also it is important to know how it works. So, Dr. Nalapat explains it as: - "MLP works with the emotional meanings of experiences, events and memories that are connected with music in one's biography and it can be used in verbal form. MLP gives opportunity to pay proper regard to both the aspects of how to combine psycho-therapeutic and socio- therapeutic work. Life panorama is a word which comes from the biographical work in integrative therapy. From the present we look back on the whole wide panorama of our life development, back into the past and forward into the anticipated future, in order to understand ourselves in our identity, in our life, in its entirety. In a course of that process, we look at individual stages of life, but always pay regard to the social context and the time we grew up.[3]

MLP (Music Life Panorama) emphasizes experience with various kinds of music that have taken an emotional significance during our life. The effect of music is always dependent on context and mood. It is linked with emotional events and periods in our lives and releases the memory and the feelings that were linked with specific situations and events in our lives at that time. Recollection of emotions in tranquillity, with the aid of music, has an important role in music therapy. If a client remembers his/her musical life panorama, it inevitably brings his/her story to life. This helps us to recreate the awareness of musical healing experiences which had been forgotten due to various life situations. In integrative music therapy, it has an active improvising component also. The process is a theragnosis (therapeutic and diagnosis together) for the music therapist in an informal way.[1]

"Music therapy," has helped in treating many people with problems like dementia, dyslexia and trauma." Many children with learning disability and poor coordination have been able to learn respond to set pieces of music. Dr. Chugh recommended a mini-synthesiser to play on for a five-year-old child who was withdrawn and unsociable with his peers because of a slight retardation. Soon, he noted a marked improvement in the child's social and interpersonal skills.[2]

The human mind is affected by music is no longer a vague notion. Dance critic Ashish Khokar cites an experiment as proof: "Music is produced from sound, and sound affects our sense perception in many ways. Even fish in an aquarium were once made to listen to different kinds of music and it was found that their movements corresponded with the beat of the music. Mind you, fish do not hear, they only felt the vibrations of the sound through water. So you can imagine what a profound effect sound and music might have on the human mind." [1]

The neural synapses pick up the electrical impulses from the brain, and then send them to every part of the body. The brain reacts to the music by releasing certain endorphins, which are said to be the natural opiates and palliatives of the body. This is substantiated by Shruti, who uses music for her healing workshops at the Gnostic Centre in Gurgaon near New Delhi, India. She reveals: "I have often found chanting or music to have a definitely positive effect on me when I have some pain or stress. It seems to soothe both the mind and the body." This is not surprising, because music often conveys mood and feeling that can be transmitted through receptors to parts of the brain that deal with the emotions. [2]

Perhaps the best example of healing through music is Swami Ganapati Sahchidananada, the pontiff of Datta Peetham in Mysore, India, who gives musical concerts for meditation and healing.

Founded on Raga RaginiVidya (knowledge of Indian classical music) and Raga Chikitsa (therapy based on Indian classical music), his concerts transmit the spiritual energy from his music to the listeners. The philosophy of his healing technique is based on the Hindu concept of the AkashaTattva (ether) being all pervading. Thus its attribute, which is also nada (sound), is all-pervasive. The Swami preaches that meditation on Lord's name is itself a medication and an antidote for all ills. Another belief is that as food is required for the nourishment of the body, so is bhajan (devotional singing) for the mind.

Yogacharya Sri Anand, a former percussion artiste, founder of the Yoga Training Centre in Mumbai, India, and the Yoga Kultur Center in Switzerland, has been conducting research on music and healing for several years. He says: "When you eliminate the beat and boom from a composition, you get pure music."[1]

He calls this music a kind of metaphysical tranquilizer. Yoga-nidra, the ancient system of inner conscious relaxation is a typical example of the power of fusion music. He explains this further in medical terms: "Heart ailments, high or low blood pressure and respiratory problems are disorders brought about by physical disharmony. Music restores harmony and thus health."

Music which resonates with the seven charkas of the body can thus energize and retune the body. In fact, the Yogacharya's experiments with the Swissair crew in helping them regulate sleep patterns after long flights and jet-lag have shown that music therapy can help the body relax to quite an extent.

Music, like some other alternative therapies, must work through the mind. The chanting of certain mantras or choir chants create vibrations within the vocal cords, which move deeper through the whole body. These vibrations must be felt in totality for them to have any effect. Hence meditation techniques, whether they are eastern or western, always use chants or music. Shruti gives an interesting example to support this: The raga (in Indian classical music, ragas and raginis are different permutations and combinations of the seven basic musical notes and their variations) Miya Ki Malhar is for the monsoon season, when the grey clouds are just about to burst. It begins on a tense note, and ends in a crescendo of sounds. Thus, if played near a person who is emotionally charged up, it will help that person release pent-up energies and negative emotions."[1]

According to Swami Ganapati Sachchidananda: "The principle underlying music therapy is, that the physical health results from a healthy mind. The right type of music helps a person relax by soothing the nerves." Perhaps that is really the most effective way in which music helps us by generating positive endorphins and easing many stress induced symptoms caused by a depletion of the energy within a person. Shruti adds that it can work to cleanse the emotional and spiritual system. Anand Avinash, founder of the Neuro Linguistic Consciousness workshop has researched music therapy and says:

> "The mystics and saints from ancient to modern times have shown how music can kindle the higher centres of the mind and enhance quality of life."[2]

Mantras, or chants used in the West, repeated monotonously, help the mind to achieve a sense of balance. The combination of sounds in Sanskrit mantras produces certain positive vibrations and elevates the mind to a higher level of consciousness.

According to Shruti: "We all know that meditation cleanses the system of negative energies and vibrations. And music is a powerful aid to meditation. In my workshops, I use music to make people more aware of their moods and feelings. I ask people to lie down and empty their minds and then listen to the music which I keep changing so that they can fit through different emotions and states of consciousness. Initially, I play genres which people can identify with such as rock, pop and film music.

Then I work my way up to quieter music. By the time they are totally relaxed, I play what you could loosely term as New Age music or music for meditation, I am especially fond of Tibetan bowl music. I have noticed that after these sessions, many people feel much energized. The whole process helps them become aware of their own emotional state."[1]

Role of Music Therapy in healing the Mankind

Music is a part of the cycle of natural life. Music is based on rhythm and harmony. Human life is based on rhythm. Day and night, seasonal changes, and all physiological and biological functions are rhythmic. We inhale and exhale, our hearts beat in systole (contraction) and diastole (expansion or relaxation.) Sleeping, eating, menstrual cycles, walking, talking, and other, if not all, functions of life are rhythmic.

We admire oratory eloquence because its rhythm and cadence, along with the words carefully chosen to awaken, inform, or appeal to our inner desires and thoughts, are harmonic and orderly. One might conclude that man is really made of rhythm; so is nature, and so is music. Man, nature, and music are made of the same ingredients.[2]

Music affects us all. We sing with it and dance to it. We accompany our most important rituals with music. We sing hymns to our Gods and pen anthems for our nations. There is no culture in the history of mankind that has not had music. Science has always tried to explain music, to tell us why and how it affects us so.[3]

There are uncountable devoted music seekers, composers, mystics, sufi saints dedicated their lives in India as well as all over the world since centuries to bring out the hidden secret powers, magic of music. But, they still remained un-conclusively. However their great lives sacrifices never went in-vain. Their life-long inventions certainly put light on marvelous revelations to the entire mankind.

Utility of music has a long history dating back to ancient orphic school in Greece. Pythagoras, Plato and Aristotle were aware of the prophylactic and therapeutic powers. There are proofs that music therapy was used by king David is said to have cured an illness by playing on the harp. Hippocrates, the father of modern medicine used music to cure human diseases. In ancient Egypt music was used to lessen the pain of women during child birth. In India music therapy has been in use for years a scientific method of effective cures of disease through the power of music.[1]

Why repeatedly mentioned mystique word to refer 'Music' is, it has got unlimited, invisible, astonishing mesmerizing healing, Curing, empowering, inspiring, creative, enthralling characteristics with its embedded melodies. Because of its amazing applications its utility is known on music therapy. Now, let us see the amazing unlimited abilities of mystique music.

Entertainment Benefits of Music: Music takes us to great entertainment and pleasure. It makes our hearts lighterand Lifts some of us to the top of the world. Great melody music enthralls all of us and moves others to tears. Really it is the only thing which touches all sensitive souls. In fact it is only the music touches the deepest chord in us and takes you to the

---

divine experience of heaven on earth for a few unexplained thrill moments in life.[1]

Inspiration And Creativity Benefits Of Music: Live silence music is well known for making our good moods. It is the great inspirer in creating new ideas. Music is the great helper for creativity in inventing new ideas.

Music Relation with Spirituality: Music is omnipresent music is holy, music is god, no prayer whichever it may be the religion, without music, no prayer is complete. So every religion, indirectly every individual life is incomplete without music.

Benefits Of Music As Healer: Music restores, maintains and improves emotional, physiological and psychological well being. Music can eliminate all kinds of impediments, blockages, and retention/stagnation of bodily fluids. It releases tension. It has been found effective in reducing gallstones, kidney stones, various inflammations, arthritis of the muscle and joints, menstrual and spastic cramps. It loosens the bowels, cleans the urinary track, and helps in reducing the pain. The glandular system stimulates and thus body releases vital healing hormones, which ultimately fight against stress related diseases such as depression, hyperacidity and various mental illnesses. The thalamus, the nerve centre of all our sensations and emotions is positively activated by the concord of music sounds. It sets of parallel reactions in the brains cortex - place of thought and reason reside to boost. To soothe frayed nerves of patients and surgeons classical music is allowed in the labor rooms and operation theatre, expectant mothers report easier delivery. Now born babies cry less. The anesthetic administration works more effectively when combined with music in operation theatre. Music abnormally, is effective in case of mental disorders. In a rare case chronic stomach ailment has prescribed a long play recording of Bach's fugues told to listen after metal and the patient did not return with any complaint later. Women undergoing hysterectomies under general anesthesia, who listened to relaxing music and sound of ocean waves, experienced less pain and were less fatigued.[1]

Endless Applications of Mystic Music: Constantly Crying babies and Children are lulled to sleep with music. Muscles actively participating in music are invisibly exercised ones become more powerful. Music can be appropriately used for dumb half developed brains and patients of hysteria. Their power to think can be in increased. Music can also be used for social contacts. Music can be very useful to introverts reserved natured people can develop in a multidimensional manner with the help of music. Music makes a man feel completely in himself. Through music self expression also can be developed. Since music is not fatal or harmful it is not necessary to keep mental patients in special custody. For mental tension patients music serves as miracle medicine. Music is the most meaningful means for mental relaxation. Music also used to train children through rhymes. It also used to train mental patients in rhythms and can be kept them busy learning music. People with less developed brains can be trained in music for entertainment of patients in hospitals. Criminals, antisocial elements in jails can be easily diverted to the precious joyful values of life by mean of melodious music. Music can alter our bodily functions, our emotions, our mind, thinking and even our behaviour.[2] It alters our pulse, BP, breathing rate skin resistance, hormone levels and so on. Appropriate music can reduce the dose of medicine required in the

---

treatment of anxiety, mild form of depression, panic attacks and migraine. It reduces the dose of pain killers needed while treating cancer pain, post operative pain and trauma wards. Music has successfully helped manage pain in dental clinics. Caesarean operations are reduced in clinics which use music in child birth. Exercising to music is another benefit. To those people who hate exercise, music makes it enjoyable.In physiotherapy centers, weight reducing clinics, schools and aerobic exercising classes music is used. In the West, couples with relationship problems, students with depressive disorders and suicidal tendencies have opened up and revealed their dilemmas after started practicing music therapy. Music therapy has helped physically challenged children develop social skills.

Nature is The Origin of Mystique Music: Music exists in a bird's voice. Wind makes rhythmic music. Music exists in river flow, waterfalls as well as sea waves, rain creates rhythmic music.

Fascinating Faces of Music: Music can sadden and frighten example as dear the music played in tragedies or horror films. It can calm and soothe as do chanting of Vedic mantras and soft instrumental music; it can excite as does the pop music, can entertain like our melodious film songs; music can elevate and uplift you to a higher state of consciousness and mental relaxation as does bhajans and devotional music; it can burst out stress effectively when devotional songs are sung in groups. [1]

Influence of Music in Animals and Plants:Even snakes like Cobra is attracted by music. Animals like horse dances for music. Hindu mythology it is well known that Krishna's flute music attracted crowd of cows. Milking cows give more milk while listening music. Music makes plant yield more.

Awareness Tips On Music Therapy: Now let us see centuries long dedicated research on music of numerous music saints concluded for the immense curing benefits to the entire mankind. Here are the names of Indian Music ragas and their diseases curing abilities. Raga Ananda Bhairawi: reduces nose related problems, Raga Kannada: helps in reducing belly and body weight; Kanachu: Wisdom inducer, Kambroji and Saaver : stomach related diseases; Kamavardhini :Kharaharpriya, NataBegada, Madhyamavathi, Mayamalavakagata, Yadukulakambhoji, Ritigala, Sriraga, Surati: All disease curers, Kedara, Chakravaka, Mukhari, Vasanta, Hussaini: Mind related diseases. Janjooti: Keeps mind ever happy, Thodi: Heart problems. Devagardhari: breath related problems; Dhanyasi: Head related diseases, Nayaki: brain related diseases, Narayana goula, Sahana, Sama, Sourastra: blesses peace of mind. Punnagavarali: skin related diseases; Poorvikalyani: eye related diseases, Bilahari: cleans soul, calms mind, Hamsadhwani: all nerves related diseases; Hindda: problems related to fear ful /horro dreams; Kedara: all throat diseases. The research on music is never ending and it is going on and goes for ever.

With so many unlimited benefits there is no doubt that calling music as divine or god. Now certainly we can call 'MUSIC' is the elaboration form of 'MYSTIC UNIVERSAL SPIRITUAL INVISIBLE CUROR'. Now, let the entire humanity realize the healing powers of music and practice half an hour daily to forget all worries always enjoy all merrier with mankind's merciful divine music.[1]

Dr. Suvarna Nalapat has beautifully mentioned the effects of the art music as a therapy in our lives: "Music as a science decreases the basal metabolic rate, respiratory rate, blood pressure, anxiety and tension, is antidepressant, reduce pain by increasing the secretion of endorphin from the nerve cells. As an art it gives the greatest and the finest aesthetic (and anesthetic) effect relieving all the pains this life has imposed on us."[1]

Music therapy supports the groups for children, and for the relatives of patients also is useful. The former for personality development of the new generation of citizens, the latter for relieving the stressful experience of having a beloved one at home/or in the hospital.[2]

Listening to classical music stimulates the temporal lobe of the brain and gives peace and ecstasy simultaneously. It gives more concentration power and increases one's efficiency at workplace. Listening to music activates symmetry operations associated with higher brain functions so that, a regular music listener become an intellectual. On the other hand, the heavy metal music, lyrics of hate and despair are destructive to brain cells. What the children hear may destroy them permanently.[3]

All of us begin our life as musical infants enjoying the *layayoga of the* maternal rhythmof heartbeat and her loving crooning and lullaby. The stressful and strenuous life makes us forget this experience of bliss. Music therapy brings back this loving tender care of mother-nature back to the people who need it. The basic of music therapy is that it is not only part of our culture but also part of our nature. By promoting our culture and our nature we are healing ourselves of all the discrepancies and diseases that have crept into our beautiful lives and society.

Music is ultimately the spiritual energy in the human race and harnessing it with the cosmic energy (God) the *laya-yoga* between *jivatma* and *parmatma* happens, which cures all the illness of the world and makes it a better place to live in, in peace and harmonies.[1]

After such deep thoughts on the effects of music on human life, we can say that music really has a vital role to play in the course of present and till eternity, as it is actually eternal.

CHAPTER – 4

The contribution of Indian Music to Music Therapy

- *The power of Sound.*
- *Self realization – the 'Goal of Hinduism'.*
- *Role of different forms of Indian Music in 'Healing Process'.*
- *The Power of "AUM"- Vibration defining the entire Cosmos.*

CHAPTER 4

THE CONTRIBUTION OF INDIAN MUSIC TO MUSIC THERAPY

Health according to definition of WHO, is not merely the lack of disease. The mental, spiritual and intellectual health also has to be taken into consideration.[1]

The Yajnavalkya Smriti mentions:

> "Veenavadhanatathvangnasruti, jathi, visarthatalanjaaprayasena moksha margamniyachathi"

i.e. the one who is well versed in veena, one who has the knowledge of shrutis and one who is adept in tala, attains salvation without doubt.

The primitive people sang and danced when they felt something positive to express and enjoy. Singing and dancing were, therefore, the spontaneous outbursts of their simple and sweet thoughts. To observe time and to create stirring emotion they clapped hands, nodded their heads and moved their limbs. They very much loved love songs, erotic songs, and animal songs, hunting songs, raining songs, war songs and the songs of lamentation, songs of medicine and weather charms.[2]

Musical experiences which human beings experience are called 'MLP' (musical life panorama).[3] Now in context to music therapy it is essential to know the meaning of the term 'MLP' and also it is important to know how it works. So, Dr. Nalapat explains it as:- "MLP works with the emotional meanings of experiences, events and memories that are connected with music in one's biography and it can be used in verbal form. MLP gives opportunity to pay proper regard to both the aspects of how to combine psycho-therapeutic and socio- therapeutic work. Life panorama is a word which comes from the biographical work in integrative therapy. From the present we look back on the whole wide panorama of our life development, back into the past and forward into the anticipated future, in order to understand ourselves in our identity, in our life, in its entirety. In a course of that process, we look at individual stages of life, but always pay regard to the social context and the time we grew up.[1]

Music has immense power to change one's life. It has almost every single expression which we usually hide from others, which we don't like to be conveyed even through our eyes, which we don't like others to get idea of. But, it doesn't mean that Music would harm anyone by letting their secrets being public. Rather, it has every small possibility of giving unique strength to a person of getting the access to his roots and to touch the roof of his/her life. In our very own country India, music has always been the great source of expression & expansion. Be it the rhythm, the melody, the harmony, literature or the occasion. Music has always served & solved all the purposes being one single outstanding term. As per my opinion the definition of music comprises a meaning in it which is – Masses of unanimity stands for intellectual civilization. And this meaning tells the whole story. Now, this is a tough task to do justice to this specific and straight meaning. But then where there's a will there's a way, so, here, there will be an effort on the Researcher's part to explain & prove what comes on her mind & what her heart feels about Music.

Music in India did not originate from a single place, city or state. This is what we have been told to on the historical grounds. Music has grown with the passage of time. We cannot even say that it took birth in our country. Though it has been fed and well-nourished by us (the Indians), from the ancient times. And this fed child became a boom, not only for our country but for other nations & purposes. Music is just like a tree spreading its arms all around to cover all of us, first of all to entertain & excite, then to calm & relax.

The power of Sound

"Chaitanyamsarvbhootanamvivrtamjagadatmana|
Naadbrahmtadanandamdwitiyamupasmahe||1||
Naadopasanyadevahbrahmavishnumaheshwarah|
Bhavantyupasitanoonamyasmaadetetadatmakah||2||"

I.e. the actual form of sound is 'Divine' consciousness, and the unmanifested consciousness is divided into two principles i.e. Shiva and Shakti. The whole manifestation of the universe remains latent as the casual form in the bosom of 'Prakriti' (i.e. Shakti) which is termed as 'Shakti'. It is regarded that there is a friction between Prana and Fire. This creates energy through which the sound is produced, and that becomes the basis of music.

Music finds an expression only through the medium of 'Sound'. Music has been defined as an art of combining sounds, which are agreeable to the ear. This sound is the effect on the ear of a wave like motion of an elastic medium caused by vibrations. Now the vibrations imp rings on the ear drum and set up a nervous disturbance which we call 'Sound'. To hear a sound we need a vibrating object as well as a receiver. The vibration object transmits the sound waves and the receiver (ear) absorbs the energy passed through the vibrating object. During this process the elastic medium such as air or water works as a mediator. For example, if a bell is rung inside a jar from which air has been extracted by means of air pump, the sound of the bell cannot be heard, so, a medium is necessary for hearing a sound.

This production of sound is an essential element and forms the groundwork of music. As Pt. Sharangadeva says about the production of sound:

"Nakaramprananamaanamdakaramanalamviduh|
Jatahpranavinsyogatteninadoabhidhiyate||

It means that 'Na' is for vital air and 'Da' is for vital heat. Thus it is clear that sound or Nada is the result of the united action of the vital air and the vital heat of the body. The sound thus produced viz. Mandra the chest, Madhya the throat and Tar the head.[1]

The sound thus produced is directly connected with soul and is known as 'OM' or 'NADA BRAHMA'.[2]

In the 9th-11th century A.D., the concept of the casual sound was expressed in a clear way. In Sangitasamayasara, we find that the casual sound (nada) has been defined as Brahma, Vishnu and Maheshvara:

"Naadaatmaanastrayodevaabrahmaa-vishnu-maheshvarah"

Matanga has emphasized upon the importance of Nada, i.e.
"Idanimsampravyakshyaminadalakshanamuttamam|
Na naadenbinageetamnanaadenbinaswarah|
Na naadenbinanrittamtasmanunaadatmakamjagat||

Matanga has also described the five grades of sound units from basic sound as:

"Nadoyamnadaterdhatohsa cha panch-vidhobhavet|
Sukshma-chaivatisukshmaschavyaktovyaktaschakritrimah||"

That is, sukshma, atisukshama, vyakta, avyakta and kritrima (subtle, most subtle, manifested, unmanifested and artificial) sound, evolved from the nada. The sukshma or subtle sound is known as 'guhaavaasi' i.e. residing in the depth of the subconscious mind, and when it manifests itself in the breast (hridaya), it comes to be known as atisukshma or most subtle. Again, when the sound is manifested in the throat (kantha), it becomes vyakta or manifested, and when it is evolved in the palate, it is known as avyakta or unmanifested, and when it is manifested in the mouth, it is known as artificial.[1]

All that exists is the product of Nada. Our tradition teaches us that sound is God the Nadabrahma. It means that musical sound is the step to the realization of self.

A Nada is of two kinds:-

• Ahata Nada.

• Anahata Nada.

Ahata nada is caused by physical impact. It is called struck sound. It can be perceived through ears. The creation of music is concerned with Ahata Nada.

Anahata Nada is not produced by physical impact. It is called unstuck sound. It is experienced by yogis. The perception of music is concerned with Anahata Nada.

The sound has been the biggest power in context of music. Scientifically, sound is the base of the building called "MUSIC". In Indian Music Nada have two varieties which are:-Aahat and Anahat Nada. Aahat is the one which is connected and well knitted with music. Aahat has three qualities, which are pitch, timbre and intensity. Though, socially sound is everywhere from a crying baby to a singing lady, from an animal roaring to a saint preaching. But basically when we talk about music & sound then Sound has its own particular character which is suitable to the melody and feel of Music. 'Nada' is the term used in music for sound and it is said that the sound which is suitable for music is called Nada. That particularly characterized sound has immense power and importance in music. While talking about Music therapy, we must establish one statement clearly that therapy which so ever it is, has certain rules and the requirements for its implementation. For Music therapy, Sound is the base and the repetitive sound, that too musically useful is the wall which can provide a living body with a beautiful and sound four walls of peace, self-enlightenment, confidence and power.

It is a well-known fact that a musical note pleases the ear while a noise displeases it. Let us see why it is so. The difference between a musical sound and a noise consists in the fact that the former arises from 'regular vibrations' of the air. The only cause that is more essential to give rise to agreeableness is regularity. Regularity is the order of nature. The planets move around the sun in regularity. They also move round their own axes in regularity. The years roll by in regularity. The seasons, the tides, the day and the night, all come and go in regularity. Man's birth and death take place in regularity. Youth and old age, and their millions of organic changes, exhibit themselves in regularity, and, in fact the plant life and the animal life are bound up in their growth and development by strict rules of regularity, obedience to which means pleasure, while disobedience causes pain. What a grand power is regularity!

Again, embryology teaches us that in the mother's womb the nervous system develop much earlier than the heart, which begins to beat in the third or fourth month. It is again a work of regularity. The heart propels blood throughout the body, and by means of arterial pulsation the whole nervous system is drilled into a discipline of regularity. The soft nervous substance is so much lined with regular impressions, that every impulse coming from outside in regularity is received agreeably and every irregular impact causes an inconvenient displacement of the molecules of the nerves, and gives rise to a feeling of disagreeableness. Hence a musical sound originating from regular vibrations pleases the ear, while a noise displeases it.

When we are discussing the power of Sound in context of Music, then first of all we must know that how do we acquire the use of music as a language for expression and communication? To the younger version of our selves, language is music. A new born hears a symphony of diverse abstract sounds; language has not yet become representational. "The infant lacks the capacity of relating to language as a semantic system, to its symbols and concepts, he is responding to the various sound components – intensity, pitch, rhythm and timbre...If we could turn back and identify with the infant, hearing the wood around us through infantile ears, might not be the secrets of music unveil themselves before us, enabling us to understand its paths of expression?"[1]

The infant cannot comprehend specific meaning in verbal communication, but the "inarticulate, preverbal music of mood and intent is a constant undercurrent in speech"[2]. Words are nothing more than sounds arranged in patterns, and yet the infant recognizes the essential import of these patterns, and that the patterns have significance. This attachment of significance to sound patterns precedes actual comprehension. It is the repetition of sound patterns which reinforce the pattern's particular significance. The very act of repetition serves as a link between the parent and child, a notice of regularity.

This early mode of expression and communication between parent and child creates within us the latent ability to utilize sounds as meaningful expression. Just as the parent assists the newborn, the music therapist helps the new client to feel comfortable using the elements of music for expression and communication. And, in this context music is primarily a language of feelings and emotions, common to man, the brute and inanimate nature. Corresponding to the word-language, it has, as a science, its own alphabets, its own words, grammar and literature; and as an art, its own pleasing elements of beauty.

'Father Schmidt' and 'Carl Stumpf' are of opinion that music evolved like speech "from the need to give signals by sound". It has been mentioned in the Vedic literature that music evolved out of the rics or stanzas (mantras) of the Rigveda, set to tunes i.e. tones. So, the Samaveda, being a collection of rics or stanzas, is regarded as the source of Indian music, nay, of the music of the world.[1]

The psycho-analysts and the psychologists are of opinion that speech and music have originated from a common source, and the primitive music was neither speaking nor singing, but something of both.[2]

Sound in relation to music reveals another truth. This is discovered in ancient India that there are seven basic musical notes, which were derived from sounds of nature or songs of various animals. Through meditation, we can feel that each note corresponds to a certain chakra, or energy wheel, within us. The chakra becomes activated when the frequency of the note matches that of the corresponding chakra and can be strengthened by it. By using the notes in certain combinations, the connection between the chakras is also activated.

In Indian music SA – the root note- corresponds to the Mooladhara, the chakra at the base of the spine. This is the protector of the subtle system and therefore SA is present in all the scales and is constant. Four notes in the Indian scale can be sharpened, or lowered – RE (2nd), GA (3rd), DHA (6th), NI (7th). One note can be sharpened, or raised MA (4th). PA (5th) is also a constant like SA. By using mantras, or affirmations, we not only invoke the qualities of the chakras with the name of the deity present at that chakra, but we can also use the notes that give the strongest effect.

The Indian literature, both Vedic-Epic and Classical, have described that music originated from the sound (nada), which is the product of ether (akasha):

"shabdaakasha-sambhava"

Sound originates in the living beings, from the friction of air (prana-vayu or the vital air) and heat-energy (agni=wil power). It evolves first in a casual form (anahata) and then in a gross form (ahata). When the gross sound emanates from the vocal-chord, it is called sound, and when again it is sweet and soothing, it is called music or sangitam.[1]

In our day-to-day life, we find that all the seven chakras are not active all the time. Some do not work properly, as there are some hindrances, due to lack of required energy power. Since these chakras are connected with different organs, any hindrance in their functioning creates physical imbalance in the person. Emotional and mental imbalances are also seen depending upon the state of the chakras.

In speaking of the effect of sound, Mr. Alain Danielou is of opinion that: 'we must be aware of the difference between organized sounds and what is generally called music.'[2]

He further mentions: when certain systems of music like western music for example, give up the fundamental accuracy of natural intervals by adopting such compromises as equal temperament, they entirely forego any possible "magical" effects, and, indeed, also most of its emotive power. Such music is bound to become more and more abstract. Despite a few reformers are ever ready to imitate western mistakes, the higher forms of Indian music still lay stress on accuracy and, as such, represent the most scientific system of music in existence today.[1]

Physics tells us that the atom of a given substance is merely a particular arrangement of a given number of electrons. This number is the key to the very nature of that substance, and all its physical properties are connected with it. In music, on the other hand we find the same number or relation and study its properties, but we can also experience its effect as an emotion. We can discover its thought value, create the link between number and idea and thus reach the very casual substratum (basic rock) of all things, which is part of nature of thought, as several modern physicists believe. This had also been envisaged (foreseen) by the ancient seers of India. 'Nada' the primordial vibration, the rhythmic movement within the divine mind, is the cause of all that exists.[2]

The different forms of existence are but the results of different tattvas, the different elements within the undifferentiated basic continuum."[3] He also has a strong opinion about the vibration of the sound and he states: - "any sound with vibrato, such as that produced by most western violinists, which is a constant movement between two very close sounds, produces its own jamming of harmonics and can therefore have no profound effect. In this case too, the classical Indian Vocal and Instrumental technique is much superior, since it aims at pure unwavering sounds and at a precise pitch. The effect of such sounds is much deeper and more lasting." He also comments on the pitch and intervals in context of Indian classical music as follows: - "In Indian classical music, pitch and interval are strictly connected. This means that, in performing a raga, once the 'Sa', or drone, has been given, the 3rd, the4th, the 5th, all the intervals will always be at the same pitch.This must be emphasized because it is not the case in other systems of music. Whenever the same interval, the same note appears, it will be of exactly the same frequency. It will therefore strike our nervous system in exactly the same place and, like a little hammer striking again and again, it will gradually make that place so sensitive that even unmusical people, or those not listening, or even animals, will be affected and moved in that particular area of their sensibility. Hence the power of Indian music is extremely great, as was that of ancient Greek music. This power is unknown, because it does not exist in other systems of music."

Indian music consequently hasbeen an ideal field for research into the theory of sound. Even today however classical Indian Music offers the most magnificent example of the lines along which scientific music can work. Any systematic study and repeat experiences however have to rely on mechanical instruments to produce the desired pitch and intervals with rigorous precision for any length of time and at the desired intensity. Only then can successful experiments on living beings and inanimate matter can be conducted. These are bound to produce amazing results and lead to a complete revision of modern theories on music and will most probably confirm much of what the Indian sages postulated long ago.[1]

When this term 'long ago' comes on the mind, in that case it is very important to mention the origin of Shrutis in context of the Sound. As shrutis, also known as microtones were the twenty- two nadas, which formed the basic ground for the extension of the Indian Music.

The microtones (shrutis) are the minute perceptible (shravanyogya) tones or musical sound-units that constitute the structures of seven tones likeshadja, rishabha, gandhara, madhyama, panchama, dhaivata and nishada (corresponding Vedic tones, chaturtha, mandra, atisvarya, krushta, prathama, dvitiya, tritiya). The shastrakaras (authors of Indian music) have defined 'shrutis' as:

"Prathamahshravanatshabdahshruyatehrasvamatrakaha|

Sashrutihsamparijneyasvaravayavalakshamanam||"[1]

The use of microtones may properly be assigned to the beginning of the classical period in the 600-500 B.C. when the laukika gandharva type of systematic-cum-scientific music was gaining ascendency.

Bharata has systematically determined and arranged 22 microtones on the basis of those 5 basic minute tones- dipta, ayata, karuna, mridu and Madhya. He termed these 5 tones as 'jatis' or adharas of the 22 microtones. The division of the shrutis, according to the jatis, is also accepted by the authors on music of the Karnatic system.

It should be remembered that all the names of the shrutis bear full significances of their own, and these significances are given according to eight aesthetic sentiments and moods (rasa and bhava). On the basis of aesthetic sentiments and moods of the 5 jatis i.e. jati-shrutis of Naradaare classified thus:

Jatis	Sentiments & moods
Dipta	Excited, bright, radiant
Ayata	Extended, broad, wide
Mridu	Soft, tender, mild, gentle
Madhya	Central, proper, tolerable, middling
Karuna	Sympathetic, compassionate, tenderness, merciful

In such a way 'Sound', in its different forms and with different names has a powerful role to play in Music and music therapy.

Self-realization – the 'Goal of Hinduism

Before we dwell on the subject of self-realization we need to understand the real meaning of gaining self-realization. For the Hindu religion, self-realization (Aatm Gyaan) is knowledge of the true self beyond both delusion and identification with material phenomena.

Dr. Suvarna Nalapat mentions: - "when we hear music, our short-term memory is active. Listening being a private and internal experience is more related to spirituality than physicality. She further mentions: - "If we listen to a person as a piece of art, or a raga in musical context, that will free us from our personal pathological view points. Listening to a person in this way is directed towards aesthetic expression, and every human being has this potential, however unmusical he/she may be, because he/she too has the species-specific order/rhythmic raga in him. She has also mentioned: - "A musical form or an art form is a musical consciousness that is visualized (pashyanti), in the creator's mind, thought upon or analyzed (madhyama) into an orderly form, and brought out (vaikhari) or communicated to others, making a dream raga come true. For this to happen, sradhha, bhakti (concentration, devotion) and sruti (listening) are needed."[1]

On the basis of above references of different opinion holders we can get an idea of the importance of Indian music in context of sound & Music therapy. As we all know that music can be heard first and then only it can be used for the healing. When we are thinking of music therapy, we should know the types of listening for the implementation of this particular therapy which has a base of sound and listening. Listening to somebody/something means we are prepared to hear it, we enjoy listening to it and we want to hear more of it. There are three basic modes of listening which are:-empirical listening, open listening and focused listening.

Empirical listening- According to the researchers it is the naïve listener who listens holistically, not the trained one. While listening, when one makes sense of the world by his/her mind influenced by the surroundings, it is called empirical listening. When non-sensory part of cognition is silent, and hence the listeners appear to be silent while they are active internally being unconscious of their own changing mental state.

Open listening- In our home, when we listen back to the session, context, time and place are changed. We are distant from the performer and the session. It confirms our intuitions and impressions that arose during the session. This open listening from different points of view gives us intuitions.

Focused listening- where there music is listened according to our manodharma, both musically and extra musically, that listening session is called focused listening.

Out of above mentioned three types or modes of listening, the focused listening is the one which can be a mean of therapeutic healing by music.[1]"

In historical roots of Indian music and its therapeutic role the focused listening has played an important role. When we talk about samgana, singing and listening of different richas of Rigveda's under Samaveda, we find that it was all based on the focused notes, focused compositions and focused style of recitation, then just because of this focus in the formulization of different stotras, shlokas and prayers those stotras, shlokas and prayers if recited properly have the power to change a personality, circumstances and physical illness. It can be a reason for which music therapy has its very roots in Indian Music.

The branch of Advait Vedaant is the one that has particularly developed a concept and According to Vedaant, God as Sat-Chit-Anand is perfect existence, consciousness, bliss. Whereas the manifest universe which is a play of Shakti or energy is temporal, the immutable principle or reality is beyond time. God is not exactly a being - in order for there to be being, there has to be non-being - and, it is said, that such dualism within the differentiated reality does not exist in that state. It cannot be described, quantified, reasoned, or explained all of which exist on a differentiated basis only directly experienced as itself. Shakti or energy, as an abstraction, is eternal but its manifestations are continually changing. Therefore, in Hinduism, God is represented in both male and female form. The male as Sat-Chit-Anand is immutable; the female Shakti is temporal. While being omnipresent and immanent in reality, Sat-Chit-Anand is formless. Shakti is manifested but, also, exists in an

---

unexpressed form inside of Sat-Chit-Anand. Therefore, even if the Universe ceases to exist at one point, it will eventually be reborn because Shakti in an immaterial form is also eternal. What motivates the action is described more poetically as a dance or a play.

Life begins with consciousness. What makes an ant different from a rock is some sense of itself. Rather than existing purely causally, it has some degree of freedom, but the grosser awareness is more causally bound. In its pure form as Sat-Chit-Anand, consciousness is said to be completely independent of causality. And therefore true freedom can only be realized in that state. Until then, the mind is bound to causal existence to greater and lesser extents. An awareness of self is present in grosser and subtler forms. Animals or even a microbe will have some form of awareness. However, in mankind, the ability to reason allows this base awareness to be refined into higher existential contemplation.

Vedanta describes the mind as being composed of sheaths or veils going from a gross awareness of self to a subtler awareness. Love - what we call love - is a very complex emotion described by as a feeling of empathy or compassion. The identification of one's self with others. According to Vedanta, selfless love is actually an attribute of the self-realized. The mind shorn of its grossness is perfectly pure and, just like water poured from a jug into a pond mingles in an undifferentiated manner, so ultimately in Nirvikalp Samadhi or enlightenment, there is a type of universal identification. This identification is not merely a delusion but actually a state of simultaneous experience. Yogis have described having a spherically expanding universal vision and a state of indescribable rapture. Scripture gives the metaphor of a voluminous lake overflowing with pure water. It is also said that "Self-realization is not easy to achieve and requires spiritual practice, sometimes over multiple life times."

One of the biggest reasons for this difficulty is that the thirst of the soul for material existence is not sated. Though realization is by far the greatest prize and the culmination of achievement, it is elusive. (Kapila, the ancient sage, stressed that self realization was much greater and much more beneficial than the gratification of one's senses.[1]

Prarabhdh, Karma, the force of accumulated metaphysical causality, the impulses whose imprints or Samskaara in the mind where the subtle most human desires are the yearnings of the soul. (The only thing that man ought to know and which brings about his final emancipation is the knowledge of true self, which is represented by the formula 'Om Tat Sat'.

Ramakrishna said that God himself has become all these forms. It is not his will that the play should come to an end. That's why self-realization is not easily achieved.

Saint Gyaaneshwar said that the play existed for the sport of God. It was all his forms and manifestations.

The yearnings or desires cause the soul to seek out new manifestations. At death, though the gross body and senses die, the causality of those desires does not die. It seeks out a new corporeal existence. If the motive force is good, then the bound soul will go to any number of heavens; if the motive force is bad, it will go into any number of hells. The place where it goes is precisely motivated by its own nature. Hell is a place where there is suffering and ignorance. Heaven is where there is pleasure or sensory enjoyment. Neither residence in that heaven or hell, for the bound soul, is permanent. The soul (Aatma), while working off its previous Karma, continually acquires new karma. Like a metal hammered with new impressions, in the course of a life, the actions we reinforce shape the quality of the mind and the subtlest part of the mind is the soul. Therefore, it is conceivable that if someone continually acquired bad karma by reinforcing bad actions they would remain in hell for a very long time. However, the soul can always be redeemed because there is the power of free will or independence from causality that originates from God himself.

Good and evil is equivalent to knowledge and ignorance. Knowledge is good. Ignorance is evil. Ignorance leads to suffering and bondage. Knowledge takes us to happiness and liberation.

The highest heaven is said to be self-realization because that state is eternal, ever new, pure, perfect, and rapturous. Therefore, it is considered to be better than any sensual heaven, such as those in the realms of the gods.

Self-realization is achieved through 4 types of spiritual practices.

- **Karma yog-** without attachment to the fruit of action, acting by offering the fruit of the action to God. In other words, the practice of wholesome actions, actions that are complete, that fulfil all aspects of the present moment, leaving one in a state of fulfilment, i.e. free from desire, until the next impulse arises. All actions have a personal component which is unavoidable, be it pleasant, neutral or unpleasant. Wholesome, harmonious or in the flow actions are by definition fulfilling and therefore lead to Self Realization.

- **Raajyog**- psychic control or one pointed meditation that first focuses thought onto one point and then stops thought leaving only the underlying awareness.

- **Bhakti yog**- the development of love for God and other beings.

- **Gyaanyog**- reasoning the mind from gross most to subtle most state culminating in Samadhi. This type of Gyaan or knowledge is not exactly like book learning. Rather Gyaan is discovering one's self and uncovering it's mysteries through direct inner contemplation. Ultimately knowledge of relative phenomena dissolves and only the original Life-Force or God remains.

In context of Hindustani Music, as the researcher thinks, first of all in Karma yog, we make a karma by choosing music for a regular practice because it has some melodic features which sooth our excitement towards the art, then we proceed further and we give music a constant thought on our minds under the Raajyog. After achieving a certain level of regular practice in music we come across the basic feel of Sangeet which is 'Brahmanand Sahodar'. And this basic feel leads us to the spiritualism under the third step of self-realization, which is Bhakti yog. In Hinduism Bhakti is the medium to achieve Gyaan or knowledge. So, in a natural process by following the first three steps of self-realization, through Hindustani music we can be able to achieve the goal of Hinduism which is the Knowledge of Self.

It is not fortuitous that Bhagwan Krishna identified himself with the Samaveda. We all know that the Indian culture has been shaped by oral tradition from the Vedic period and hence music has influenced its various manifestations naturally. It is believed that the very two pillars of any culture are literature and art, and, the musical forces which so actively controlled the Vedic phase of Indian literature were, in fact, never eradicated. Through the successive high tides and low ebbs of love for sound, taste for finer manipulations of pitches, skilled use of flexible rhythms and finally, through the longing for the abstract aesthetic identity of form and content, music continued to hold its sway. By this brief piece of information, we can elaborate this statement in a well-organized manner that the two pillars for Indian culture have been the literature and Art.

Now, coming on our topic, the performing art form, Music has been in roots of the Indian culture from the ancient times. Hindustan which has basically one religion which is "Hinduism" has followed this performing art in every single best possible way, and, the goal has always been "Self Realization". The two famous Hindu Epics, "Ramayana" and "Mahabharata" tell the whole story about the union of literature and music and the effects of music in different circumstances.

Role of different forms of Indian Music in 'HEALING PROCESS

Swara, Tala and Laya- these are the three basic elements of Sangeet (Music). It means that Sangeet is used for its three fold meaning namely; vocal music, instrumental and dancing, for example:

"Geetam vadyam tatha nrityam sangeetamuchyte"!!

- Sangeet Darpan

Sound, one of the five eternal elements of nature, termed as Nada, gave birth to Sangeet. Vocal music is prior to instrumental music and dance.

Sangeet, as a combination of above three parts pleases and soothes the minds of living beings.[1]

Pro. Sambamoorthy has said: the eternal law of music is the survival of the beautiful in the realm of lakshya or musical compositions and the survival of the useful in the realm of lakshana or musicology.[2]

The origins of Indian classical music can be found from the oldest of scriptures, part of the Hindu tradition, the Vedas. Samaveda, one of the four Vedas, describes music at length. Indian classical music has its origins as a meditation tool for attaining self-realization. All different forms of these melodies (Ragas) are believed to affect various "chakras" (energy centers, or "moods") in the path of the "Kundalini". However, there is little mention of these esoteric beliefs in Bharat's Natyashastra, the first treatise laying down the fundamental principles of drama, dance and music. The Samaveda, one of the four Vedas, was created out of Riga-Veda so that its hymns could be sung as Samagana established its first principles. Hindustani classical music has its origin as a form of meditation, though available mainly to an elite audience.

Indian classical music has one of the most complex and complete musical systems ever developed. Like Western classical music, it divides the octave into 12 semitones of which the 7 basic notes are SA Re Ga Ma Pa Dha Ni SA, in order, replacing Do Re MiFa Sol La Si Do. However, it uses the just intonation tuning (unlike Western classical music which uses the equal temperament tuning system.

Indian classical music is monophonic in nature and based around a single melody line which is played over a fixed drone. The performance is based melodically on particular ragas and rhythmically on talas.

Here are some articles on the role of Indian Music in a therapeutic manner:

As we all know that Indian music has its roots in the Vedic culture. It has evolved to the present age with its basic elements inspite of some additions and alterations in the ancient and medieval period. But the tradition of music remained same. Thus Music has been looked upon as a "Sadhna" a medium for mental uplift.

RAGA: -The melody type a component of Art Music in India

A Raga is defined in Sangeet Darpan as-

> "Yoyam dhwanivisheshastu swarvarnvibhooshitah|
> Ranjakojanchittanaam saa rag kathyate budheih||"
>
> -Sangeet Darpana

i.e. A Rag is embellished with the colour of musical notes, has its separate tune and import and is pleasing to mind.

As there is also another saying in Sanskrit- "RanjayatiitiRagah"- which means, "That, which colors the mind, is a Raga."Thus in short we can define a Raga as "a particular combination of notes with varnas having the property of pleasing the mind of a listener."The first reference of the Raga occurs in the 'Brihaddeshi', by Matanga, written sometime in between the 5th and 7th centuries A.D.[1]

The root word of the term 'Raga' is the Sanskrit word 'Ranja'. Ranja means-to please, to colour, to tinge. Each of the meanings of the root word has a content of pleasure in it. From this, it is evident that Raga essentially has a content of pleasure in it.[2]

Raga, however, has a much wider range of meaning conveying many ideas and images such as-colour, hue, tint, dye (especially red colour), redness, inflammation, any feeling or passion (especially love, affection or sympathy), vehement desire, interest, joy, delight, loveliness, beauty, a musical note, melody (musical mode or order of sound), seasoning, anger, greediness and so on.[1]

Matanga has defined seven kinds of Ragagiti in the 'Brihaddeshi'. To describe some of the salient features of these seven ragagitis, it can be said:

1. The nature of the shuddhagiti was mild. The tones (the movement of tones) were straight and stretched in three registers, mandra, madhya and tara.

2. The tones of the bhinna were crooked (i.e. undulating in movement), but subtle and possessed gamakas.

3. The tones of gaudi were closed together and the gamakas that were used, were played in three parts. The tones of the lower register (mandra) were produced with repeated sounds of a-kara and u-kara from the conjunction of chin and breast (chibhuka and vaksha).

4. The raga was rhythmic and soothing, and possessed gamakas and four varnas, and was surcharged with aesthetic sentiments and moods (rasa and bhava).

5. The tones of sadharani were straight in movement and rhythmic and were produced in rapid tempo. This giti was produced with plain kakus. The sadharani was known by the combination of all gitis.

6. The bhasha which possessed kakus and some tremulous tones was sweet and soothing.

7. The vibhasha was very pleasing to all. It was majestic and at the same time graceful. It possessed gamakas and its tones were down upto high (tara) register.

From these ragagitis numerous gramaragas evolved, and from the gramaragas, evolved bhasha, vibhasha and antarbhasha ragas.[1]

The combination of the notes following particular laws of composition and the rules of structure came to be recognized as "Rag" or the "Melody type". These "Melody types" were according to the ancient writers divided into three classes: Shudhha, Chhaya and Sankirna. The Shudhha Rag was one which was pure in the approved structure and composition of notes. The "Chhaya" was one that was to some extent influenced by the notes from other Rag. The "Sankirna" was a combination of the notes of more than one Raga.

When we talk about the term Raga, then, in fact, the vibrations of sweet sound of tones of both vocal and instrumental music create soothing and pleasing sensations or impressions is said to be the Raga. In fact a raga is more than the sensations or impressions or a bundle of impressions, and that all kinds of sound, sweet or harsh, musical or noise, create some impressions of their own, and as such it may be termed to be a Raga.[2]

Besides, the Shastrakaras have said that the ragas are possessed of some specific qualities as well as characteristics which determine them and animate them with life and energy. We thus find that the ragas have in them the musical propensities and value, which attract the mind, help to concentrate the dispersed or scattered modifications of the mind, and thus lead the audiences and lovers of music to the realm of meditation, which brings peace, joy and happiness.[1]

[2]

Ragas in relation to music therapy have a wide range of beliefs. Take for an example the Raga Bhairava. The Raga is meant to be sung or played during "Sharad" the period towards the conclusion of August to the end of September, the period during which is in India, the weather is neither too hot nor too cold. And, as it is the moderate conditions of the prevalent weather which induces peace and calm state of mind, Bhairava is, consequently, meant to be sung during this season. It should be noted, moreover, that the appropriate time for the melody being the very early part of the morning, say about five, it only accentuates the atmosphere of peaceful and calm mentality expressed by and aimed at for the Rag Bhairava. About the medicinal value of Rag Bhairava, Dr. M. Vijay Laxmi said:

"Rag Bhairava if sung or played systematically according to the scriptures possesses the following curative values:--

---

119

It cures cough, diseases of liver, regulates the action of the heart and generates vitality.[1]

Raga Shyam-kalyan helps to activate Mooladhara Chakra. It allows the Kundilini rise gently, easily and naturally.[2]

Raga Gurjari-Todi has the capacity to cool down the liver and Raga Gurjari-Todi and Yaman have the power of sustenance. Both ragas help to activate Swadisthan Chakra. Both ragas have the power to stabilize the wandering attention which is very important for the meditation.

Raga Abhogi helps to activate Nabhi Chakra and stimulate the digestion process.

Raga Bhairav and Durga have the divine bliss and protection. Both ragas help to sctivate Heart Chakra.

Raga Jaijaiwanti helps to activate Vishudhhi Chakra which controls five sense organs.[3]

Raga Bhup is found effective to purify and open the Agnya Chakra by deflating the balloon-like structures of subconscious and ego. It is also useful to release tension, anger and mental fatigue. Mood created by this raga greatly assists the kundilini to pass through the Agnya Chakra and enter the apex Chakra Sahasrara in the limbic area. The person is now in the state of thoughtless awareness.

Raga Darbari and Bhairavi are extremely helpful to settle and prolong the thoughtless awareness state. Notes of these ragas relax the limbic area.

The kundilini then soothes and nourishes the Chakra and the brain. One feels joyous, energetic, peaceful and relieved of tension and depression. The person also enjoys the sensation of cool breeze on his finger-tips. This is the state of Yoga. Regular practice in this way can open a new dimension of self-knowledge and collective consciousness.[1]

Below are some articles which talk about the important role of Ragas in healing:

The use of Raga as a therapy is the key to achieve the universal brotherhood, love, international harmony and peace; at the same time giving physical, mental, intellectual and spiritual health to all of us.[1]

Music Composition- The Prabandha: Niryukta and Aniryukta

Parshvadeva has defined prabandha as:

"chaturbhirdhatubhihshdbhishcha-angairyah
syatprabandhatet asmatprabandhah"

i.e. the gitis, which were formed of four or six music parts (dhatus), were known as prabandha.[2]

The prabandhas were again sub-divided into two classes, niryukta or nibaddha and aniryukta or anibaddha. The niryukta or nibaddha prabandha used to be measured by time-beats or talas, whereas aniryukta or anibaddha was without tala. The anibadhha was like the alapa or elaboration of the tones of a raga.

Prabandha, itself is a very detailed subject to discuss. But, from the point of view of Music Therapy, the Ela type of musical composition is of great importance as, some of the musical compositions evolved under the head of different Elas like Gana, matra, varna, varnamala, deshakhya, etc. These Ela type of musical compositions possessed chandda, alamkara and rasa.

In Music; Chandda, alamkara and rasa have their own place in attracting the mind of people so that their body can respond in a proper manner while enjoying three of them.

Different types of modern prabandha are dhamara, kheyal, tappa, thumri, dadra, gazal, kajri, rasia, bhajan, astapadi, tarana, lavani, phatka, kirtanam, gitam, ragamalika, kriti, padam, javali, tillana, svarajati, jaisvaram, varna, odam, devara, mangalam etc.

Dhrupad: Dhrupad or Dhruvapada (the rectified form of the salaga-sudadhruva-prabandha) was patronized by Raja Man Singh Tonwar (1486-1517 A.D.) and then stalwart musicians like Bakshu, Macchu, Bhanu and others of Gwaliar.[1]

Dhrupad & Dhamar

According to Faquirullah, the author of Raga Darpan, "Dhruvapad is a form composed by Raj Man Singh Tomer of Gwalior. He composed this style with the help of Nayak Bakshoo, Bhanno, Mahmood, Lohang and

Karna.[1]Dhrupad is an old style of singing, traditionally performed by male singers. It is performed with a Tambura and a Pakhawaj as instrumental accompaniments. The lyrics, some of which were written in Sanskrit centuries ago, are presently often sung in Brajbhasha, a medieval form of North and East Indian languages that was spoken in Eastern India.

The rudraveena, an ancient string instrument, is used in instrumental music in dhrupad. Dhrupad music is primarily devotional in theme and content. The great Indian musician Tansen sang in the dhrupad style. It contains recitals in praise of particular deities. Dhrupad compositions begin with a relatively long and acyclic nom-tom alap, A lighter form of dhrupad, to the 14-beat "Dhamartaal" is called a **Dhamar.** It is sung primarily during the festival of Holi.[2]

Khayal

Khayal literally means imagination, thought or fancy. Khayal is that vocal genre of all North Indian vocal styles which gives its performers the greatest opportunity and also the greatest challenge to display the depth and breadth of their musical knowledge and skills. Khayal has dominated the performing art for past 150 years.[3] Khayal is the genre of improvisational music, and hence it is the study of artist's creative individuality and ability to render a unique khayal at each performance.

Despite the presumed freedom in khayal singing it is structured upon three main characteristics: (i) the Raga (melodic mode), the Taal (meter) and the cheez (composition), (ii) the types of improvisation which are acceptable for Khayal such as alap, taan, boltaan and sargam, and (iii) the placement of these material for creation of aesthetically and technically balanced performance.[1]Khayal is not only a distinguished, richly evolved improvisational music genre, but also a study of cultural history of India since thirteenth century onwards. In Khayal form of gayaki, there are three variations of bandish:

Vilambit bandish: A slow and steady melodic composition, usually in largo to adagio speeds.

Madhyalaya bandish: A medium tempo melodic competition usually set in andante to allegretto speeds.

Drut bandish: A fast tempo melodic composition usually set to allegretto speed or faster.

Tarana

In the words of Thakur Jaidev Singh, an influential commentator on Indian music: Tarana was entirely an invention of Khusrau. Tarana is a Persian word meaning a song. Tillana is a corrupt form of this word. True, Khusrau had before him the example of Nirgit songs using "suskakshar" (meaningless words) and "patakshar" (mnemonic syllables of the mridang). Such songs were in vogue at least from the time of Bharat. But generally speaking, the Nirgit used hard consonants. Khusrau introduced two innovations in this form of vocal music.

Firstly, he introduced mostly Persian words with soft consonants. Secondly, he so arranged these words that they bore some sense. He also introduced a few Hindi words to complete the sense. It was only

Khusrau's genius that could arrange these words in such a way to yield some meaning. Composers after him could not succeed in doing so, and the tarana became as meaningless as the ancient Nirgit.[1]

Thumri

The Hindi word Thumri is said to be derived from the term "Thumakna" meaning an attractive gait. So, literary meaning is the song having attractive - rather sensuous, gait of melody and rhythm.

Thumri is usually sung at the end of *khayal* concerts It is said to have begun in Uttar Pradesh with the court of Nawab Wajid Ali Shah. There are three types of thumri: poorabang, Lucknavi and Punjabi thumri. The lyrics are typically in a proto-Hindi language called Brij Bhasha and are usually romantic.

Tappa

Tappa is a form of Indian semi-classical vocal music whose specialty is its rolling pace based on fast, subtle, knotty construction. It originated from the folk songs of the camel riders of Punjab and was developed as a form of classical music by Mian Ghulam Nabi Shori or Shori Mian, a court singer for Asaf-Ud-Dowlah, the Nawab of Awadh.

Chaiti

Chaiti are a semi-classical songs sung in the Hindu calendar month of Chait. These songs are rendered during the Holy month of Sri Rama Navami in March/April. It falls under light classical form of Hindustani classical music. The songs typically have the name of Lord Rama. Some of the popular singers of Chaiti are Girija Devi etc.

Kajari

Kajari derived from the Hindi word Kajra, or Kohl, is a genre of semi-classical singing, popular in Uttar Pradesh and Bihar. It is often used to describe the longing of a maiden for her lover as the black monsoon cloud come hanging in the summer skies, and the style is notably sung during the rainy season.

Ashtpadi

Ashtapadis or Ashtapadi are Indian hymns where the music has eight lines (steps) within each composition. Each ashtapadi song is set in a special raga (an Indian musical mode) and tala. It is a rhyme of eternal love and supreme devotion. The literal meaning of "ashtapadi" is "eight steps."[1]

Devotional forms of music

Devotional or religious songs are a prominent feature in the Indian system of music and include a variety of traditions. Bhajans or kirtans are Hindu devotional songs or music compositions used for worship or offering prayers.

Bhajans

Bhajans have evolved with times and include devotees like Mirabai, a mystic famous for her songs of worship for Lord Krishna. Bhajans are not just a form of worship or prayer but are meant to incite 'bhakti' or devotion and 'bhav' or feeling in both the singer and listener. While bhajans can be sung individually,

---

Keertana

"Keertana really deserves an alert and keen evaluative consideration by the aestheticians in general, music-thinkers in particular and in fact by all performers." This statement by Dr. Ashok D. Ranade proclaims the value of Keertana in its curative and communicative role as a musical therapeutic tool of Indian Music. The Keertana has a number of components. Keertana has narration. Apparently any event can be narrated. However an isolated and bare event in itself is consistently frowned upon by 'Keertankaars'. They tend to provide every event with the perspective of a story at one level or another. Treated in this manner an event always becomes a construed fact for the Keertankaar. A Keertankaar is found to employ verbal formulae like 'Once upon a time it so happened, O ye lords!' In a large measure these formulae are instances of stylistic moulds used by a performer who wishes to channelize the imagination of his audience in an effective manner. In the present instance it is also to be noted that the intermediate temporal frame suggested by the verbal formulae is an evocation, which becomes doubly effective because there is no chronological pinning down that would have restricted its appeal. Apart from the temporal setting provided, the narration and the speech are also distinguished by a repeated induction of the drone in the background. On one side the drone continues to provide support for an intoned prose-delivery and, on the other side the narration and the expression of a Keertankaar continues to stimulate the mind of its listeners. It is also important to be mentioned that In Keertana all events are hence provided with contexts. There are many ways of supplying these contexts. A context can be temporal. Thus a Keertankaar invariably tends to point out an earlier event or series of events as antecedent to the event he is focusing on. This is the reason why a Keertana so repeatedly harks back to chronological, mythological or the mythical past. Now in context to Music therapy, the stimulation created on certain musical ground which can give the listeners a thought process filled with imagination can lead them to the effective goals of emotions. If one can touch the emotions, be it sad or glad, that person gains a better understanding of how to act in a certain situation. So Keertana affects its listeners in so many ways on the musical stimulating ground or base.

In a Keertana though a story is narrated, an anecdote is dramatized or an entertaining aphorism is related. Coming to the metaphysical, ethical or the didactic text is never far out of sight. The quest of the Supreme Being, the nature of God, the indestructibility of soul and such other themes form the core of the Keertankaar's thematic repertoire. It is clear that these themes are so general that they are bound to confront every human being at one time or the other with more or less intensity. As a consequence, keertana achieves a remarkable double success.

Admittedly, Keertana was not originally intended or designed to spread the gospel of music, but it achieved the distinction of doing so (without of course neglecting to spread the spell of God!) Nevertheless the undeclared, successful dissemination of musical ideas compels attention of all music-educators and music-thinkers. It is said that no consideration of a musical tradition can be complete unless it takes into account the contributions made by the indirect channel like that of Keertana.

Folk Music

India's tradition and culture to a great extent revolves round music and spirituality. And in the ancient times, it was combined to achieve a better purpose in life. Folk music and dance however were an exception to this because here the purpose was to celebrate life for various reasons. As vast is the Indian culture, caste and communities, equally variant are the folk music present in India.[1]

There are more than fifty types of Folk music in India that has something different to offer to the audience. Folk music for Bhangra, Dandiya have fast pace tunes whereas Gharba, Koli have medium paced melody. The music set up for Lavani, moves from slow to fast. Similarly, with other folk music also there is lot of variety observed.

The musical instrument used for folk music also varies from region to region. However, the common ones are Dhol (Drums), Bansuri (Flute), Pungi (Blow Pipe), Manjeera (Hand cymbals).[2] These are the basic instruments used for folk music but the usage of each instrument may be more or less depending upon the folk dance. For instance, if it`s a Bhangra more of Dhol can be heard, if its Teratalli more of Manjeera is used and so on.

Folk music has even given musical instruments to Indian music. A popular Indian musical instrument Sarangi is said to be developed from a Rajasthan folk music instrument. The acceptability rate of Folk music is so high that even after all these years of existence; its popularity has not reduced. On the contrary, it has gained more popularity and spread out of its regional boundaries.

Bihu

Bihu is the festival of New Year of Assam falling on mid April. This is a festival of nature and mother earth where the first day is for the cows and buffalos. Second day is for the man. Bihu dances and songs accompanied by traditional drums and wind instruments are essential part of this festival.[1]

Uttarakhani Music

Uttarakhandi folk music had its root in the lap of nature. The pure and blessed music have the feel and the touch of nature and subjects related to nature. The folk music primarily is related to the various festivals, religious traditions, folk stories and simple life of the people of Uttarakhand. Thus the songs of Uttarakhand are a true reflection of the Cultural Heritage and the way people lives their lives in the Himalayas. Musical instruments used in Uttarakhand music include the dhol, damoun, turri, ransingha, dholki, daur, thali, bhankora and masakbhaja. Tabla and harmonium are also used, but to a lesser extent. The main languages are Kumaoni and Garhwali.[2]

Lavani

Lavani comes from the word Lavanya which means beauty. This is one of the most popular forms of dance and music that is practiced all over Maharashtra. It has in fact become a necessary part of the Maharashtrian folk dance performances. Traditionally, the songs are sung by female artistes, but male artistes may occasionally sing Lavanis. The dance format associated with Lavani is known as Tamasha.

Lavani is a combination of traditional song and dance, which particularly performed to the enchanting beats of 'Dholak', an drum like instrument. Dance performed by attractive women wearing nine-yard saris. They are sung in a quick tempo. Lavani originated in the arid region of Maharashtra and Madhya Pradesh.[1]

Rabindra-Sangeet

Rabindranath Tagore was a towering figure in Indian music. Writing in Bengali, he created a library of over 2,000 songs now known by Bengalis as 'rabindra-sangeet' whose form is primarily influenced by Hindustani classical, sub-classicals, Karnatic, western, bauls, bhatiyali and different folk songs of India.

Many singers in West Bengal andBangladesh base their entire careers on the singing of Tagore musical masterpieces. The national anthem of India and national anthem of Bangladesh is based on Rabindra-Sangeet.[2]

Dance: Nritya

Nandikeshvara has defined nritya and nritta in the Abhinaya Darpana thus:

"Bhavabhinaya-hinamtu nrittamityabhidhyate|
Rasabhava-vyanjanadiyuktam nrtyamityuchyate||"

That is, the type of dance which does not express moods (bhava) by means of dramatic performances (abhinaya), is called nritta, and the dance, which suggests sentiments (rasa), is called nritya.

Bharata says that the art of dancing evolved from the ecstatic dance of Lord Siva. Siva taught Tandu this art and Tandu in his turn preached it among the art-loving people.[1]

But it should be remembered that different dancing figures, with different motifs, are engraved on the railings of the Bharut, Amravati, Sanchi Stupe and on the walls of different rock-cut temples which were built before the Christian era, go to prove the antiquity of practice of the art of dancing in India.[2]

The Power of "AUM"- Vibration defining the entire COSMOS

Found first in the Vedic scriptures of Hinduism, Aum has been seen as the first manifestation of the un-manifest Brahman that resulted in the phenomenal universe. Essentially, all the cosmos stems from the vibration of the sound 'Aum' in Hindu cosmology. Indeed, so sacred is it, that it is prefixed and suffixed to all Hindu mantras and incantations. It is undoubtedly the most representative symbol of Hinduism.

OM or AUM is the most important and significant word of Mantra tradition. It is considered as the root mantra of all mantras. In a majority of Mantras, you will find OM. OM is the most often chanted sound among all the sacred sounds on earth. This sound is considered as the sound of the existence.[1]

It is believed that the whole universe, in its fundamental form is made up of vibrating, pulsating energy. Om is considered as the humming sound of this cosmic energy.

OM is said to be the original primordial creative sound from which the entire universe have manifested. It is also known as the 'Anahat Nada', the "Un-struck Sound". This means the sound that is not made by two things striking together. If you observe the nature of sound you'll find that all ordinary audible sound are produced by the striking of two objects : bow and strings, drum and stick, two vocal cords, waves against the shore, winds against the leaves, bat against the ball, tyres against the road etc. In short all sounds within our range of listening are produces by things visible or invisible, striking each other or vibrating together, resulting in pulsating waves of air molecules which we interprets as sound.[2]

In contrast to the above, OM is the sound which is not the result of the striking of two objects. Rather it emanates on its own. It is the primal sound of the universe that contains all sounds in itself.

The meaning of OM

Well unlike all other mantra, there is no meaning of OM. It is actually not a word, it is a sound. As per Hindu tradition, OM is the purest name of

---

God. It is the sound of the supreme consciousness. So when you repeat OM, you actually take the name of God.

Now without going into the further philosophical explanation of OM, let us learn how to meditate using OM. Repetition of OM or AUM dissolves the mind it its divine source. The chanting of OM several time loud, purifies the atmosphere.

It is believed that: "Chanting the OM mantra for 15 minutes daily can produce remarkable effect in you. This mantra will help you to calm the mind, settled the thought process and realize the self."[1]

All kinds of material sound, produced by the human organs, are really the outcome of the universal sound "OM". This universal sound exists in the atmosphere and in the ether and that can only by the yogis.

Rikis sung as Sam. Anuvakya 8 of Taittariya says: everything is Brahma. Everything is pranava, "OM". Everyone utter this word, "OM". We hear. Everyone sing Sam as "OM". All sciences teach "OM". Adhiryu chant pratihara as "OM". Agnohotra is done as "OM". Whoever wants to reach Brahma, reaches him through singing pranava, "OM".[2]

Now, this statement "Whoever wants to reach Brahma, reaches him through singing pranava, "OM", in itself is very much comprehensive about the relationship of Music with Aum. And one more thing is common that, on one hand, **if a person wants to reach Brahma, he has to sing Aum**; and on the other hand, sangeet-saadhna takes one to **"Bramhanand Sahodar"**. So, Aum is the vibration which defines the entire cosmos and music is all around.

CHAPTER – 5

Formal & Informal Research done in the field of Music Therapy (In India and Abroad)

- *Music Therapy in India.*
- *Music Therapy Round the Globe.*

CHAPTER 5

RESEARCH DONE ON MUSIC THERAPY (IN INDIA AND ABROAD)

MUSIC THERAPY IN INDIA

India known as a country of rich cultural heritage has Music in its routes. As, in the first chapter of this research work, the significant history and development of Indian music has already been discussed and the therapeutic role of Indian music has also been discussed in the later chapter, along with that, we have also discussed different definitions, structures and implementations of Music Therapy by the scholarly concerned people.

So, now, let us take a glance on different people working on Music Therapy and taking the further research in the same zone, so that we can have a clear idea about that how far in India the structure of Music therapy in based on Indian Classical Music.

The works in Music therapy in India are being steered by various scholars, & institutions. I am trying to cast some light on these works on Music therapy on Indian counterpart. The Individuals that have given their precious time in new researches for the expansion of music therapy in India are as follows.

Pt. Shashank Katti

Dr. M. Hari Haaren

Dr. Bhaskar Khandekar

Dr. Mythily Thirumalachari

Mrs. Rajasree Mukherjee

Pt. Shashank Katti

Pt. Shashank Katti born in a family of musicians is a reputed, well-known Sitar player of Mumbai. His late grandfather was a 'Kirtankar' and mother Mrs. Vimal Katti was a classical singer of her time. Naturally, music has been flowing in his blood from his birth. Besides being a professional musician he is also an electrical engineer.

He started learning vocal classical music under his mother for 10 years and continued it under the guidance of Pt. Y B Joshi for one year. Then he turned to Sitar when he was 16 years old. He started his initial lessons in Sitar from Pt. Baburao Kulkarni. After that Pt. Kamlakar Bhatawdekar - a renowned flutist and also disciple of Sitar maestro Ustad Vilayat Khan Saheb, taught young Shashank the most important 'Gaykee Ang' and turned him into a fine artist.

He was awarded 'Sumani' by 'Sursinger Sansad'. He is an 'A' grade national artist of A.I.R. and is well recognized by music lovers all over by his regular performances on A.I.R. and Doordarshan. He is 'Sangeet Visharad' of Akhil Bharateeya Gandharva Mahamandal. He is an approved composer of A.I.R. and Doordarshan. He has worked with many recording companies like Venus Records, HMV, T-Series, and Times Music etc. He was appointed as an expert in documentary film 'Gandharvaveda' based on Music Therapy and produced by Films Division.

He has been found unfolding the traditional Hindustani Ragas in the most authentic form in 'Gaykee Ang' with subtlety and originality in all his recent concerts. His concerts are, no wonder, applauded by both, press and connoisseurs.

Here are some relevant works by Pt. Shashank Katti on Music Therapy:[1]

For over a decade he has been working on 'Music Therapy on different ailments' with a team of doctors - Dr. Himalaya Pantvaidya (M.D.), Dr. Vaidya Sanjey Chhajed (M.D. - Ayurveda) & Dr. Shubhangee Dhage to develop a new therapy system called 'Sur-Sanjeevan'.

It has been observed that Sur-Sanjeevan works on diseases like Arthritis, Hypertension, Diabetes, Asthma, Insomnia, Migraine etc. Pt. Shashank Katti has developed 8 CDs under the title Sur-Sanjeevan for these ailments. He has also developed series of 8 CDs for pregnant women called as 'Garbhankur', marketed by Times Music.

He is also a music composer and is working with his brother for Venus Records. The Duo is composing music with nick name 'Shank - Neel' which is a very popular name in the music industry.

Dr. M. Hari Haaren

Dr. M. Hari Haaren is a Professional Music Therapist & healer, a cconcert performing artist, a Vocalist and CChairman of Indian Music Therapy Researcchh & Development Foundation & Society foorr Music Education, Therapy & Research, Poonndicherry, India. As a Vocalist he started his ttrraining from the age of 7 in both the systemms of Indian Music (North and South Indian TrTradition).[1] He holds a PhD in ethnomusicoloog gy from India and Hon. PhD from USA on MMuusic Therapy.

He was awarded the Rajiv Gandhi Excellence Award and the State Fine Arts Academy of Kerala for the achievements in the field of Music, Musicology. He is also the Chairman of the Society for Music Education, Therapy and Research based in Pondicherry and the Indian Music Therapy Research Foundation based in Kerala.[1]

Currently he is the Head of the College of Fine Arts and Performing Arts and Special officer for the Culture Department of the Government of Pondicherry, Pondicherry, India. He has taught at Universities in Tanjore, Mysore and Madurai in South India.

He connects his research of Music therapy with two important sensory functions which are hearing through ears and understanding through brain. In other words his music therapy program is using specially filtered classical music to improve ear and brain function. According to him by listening to the classical music one can transform the improvement of the ear function and also can recharge the cortex of the brain.

He further affirms that Music Therapy is non-invasive, non-pharmaceutical and completely safe. There are no negative side effects. Musical healing treats the cause of a listening problem by stimulating and restoring natural ear and brain function. He believes that there is an existing and gradually increasing connection between the sounds we hear and our functioning in speech, learning, energy and stress. Hearing is important because as per Dr. Haaren hearing is physical and listening is psychological.[2]

Both are vital to our communication skills, establishing good relationship, socializing with everyone and learning intuitiveness. Out of the 12 cranial

---

nerves, 10 are linked to the ear, indicating the importance of the Musical sounds to our nervous system.

Under Dr. Haaren's therapy program, the target group listens to the especially composed music and sounds through headphones while doing homework, playing, sleeping and through private listening; the music should be listened to at least 30 minutes a day for six to eight weeks preferably without break in the listening sessions.

Dr. Haaren explains: "Today, we are confronted with pollution in every sphere of life situation – be at home, school, work place, factories, office and what not. The response of the ear, brain and nervous system is to shut down in varying degrees to this onslaught Stress, strain, anxiety, depressive state of mind, restlessness all pervade our system and pulls down the existing energies." And, to fight all these problems he applies the effect of Planets and cosmology on the human body and mind for effective healing with Indian Music.[1]

He further says: "My Music which is purely classical brought out on traditional Musical instruments will not disturb the balance and equilibrium of your mind; And is very effective for healing ailments like Blood Pressure, Nervous disorder, Body Pain, Migraine, Rheumatics, stress, Anger, depression, Heart ailments, sleeplessness, and autism ; and for positive approaches to Marital harmony, Personality development, Medical Professionals, IT People, cancer Counseling, Weight loss, Diabetes, Stress Management, Children, Teenagers, Police Personals, Legal fraternity, Sports Persons, Senior Citizens etc."

With the implementation of his Music Therapy programs Dr. Haaren says: "Here is an advice to you to make the best use of my Music for early and effective healing:[1]

"Do Not listen (and I repeat DO NOT listen) to the music casually while you are engaged in driving, eating, working, cooking, chatting etc. You must listen to the music only in a relaxed position like lying down or sitting posture when you are alone or in privacy. It will be more effective if the music is heard with a Headphone. The sounds and tones of the music must get absorbed and aligned into your mind and body. Listen to the music for 20-30 minutes every day for at least 6 to 8 weeks before going to Bed."

He has composed and released 24 Audio CD's and 3 DVD's on Indian Music Therapy with Musical melodies through traditional Indian Musical instruments like Sitar, Tambura, Tabla, Veena, Violin, Flute, Santur, Mridangam, Jaltarangam etc. for Women, IT professionals, Legal Professionals, Police, Children, Heart patients, Nervous disorders, Pain Killer, Ayurveda, Yoga, Journalists, Women, 50++ age groups, Diabetes, Cancer, etc.[2]

- Indian Musical Abstract- submitted to the University Grants Commission (5 years)
- World Music Abstract- submitted to RILM, USA for approval
- Traditional Music Archives –Submitted to the Ford Foundation, USA for approval.

After having experiencing the various facets of Indian Music Dr. M. Hari Harren has now specialized in the field of Music Education and Music

Therapy wherein he finds the happiness of reaching out to somebody individually who really needs the healing touches of Indian Musical system.[1]

He is the Indian Music Therapist & Music Educationist to have attended Nine International Conferences on Music Education and Music Therapy and is a Member of the World Federation of Therapy Congress and International Society for Music Education. Dr. M. Hari Harren has visited Japan, USA, Australia, Singapore and Malaysia to practice Music Therapy for non-clinical areas.

Today Dr. M. Hari Harren is an authority of Indian Music in the National and International arena. He has written and edited (along with his Guru) more than 40 books and 50 Research papers on various aspects of Indian Music.[2] *Here are some relevant works by Dr. Haaren on Music Therapy:*[3]

Dr. Bhaskar Khandekar

(Ph.D. in Music Therapy, M.A. Violin)

His dedication towards the practical implementation of music since 1993 has established him as India's First Music Therapist, born in year 1962 in spiritual and traditional family in Jabalpur, India.[1]

Dr. Bhaskar is not only a brilliant performing artist but also an eminent educationalist having more than 25 years Teaching Experience of Indian Classical Music. Dr. Bhaskar has also given powerful play-back-music for many theatres and dramas entitling him as wonderful composer. He has given many successful Performances & Lecture-Demos & workshops on Music Therapy and received wide appreciation all over India.[2]

In his Second Phase - Dr. Bhaskar Khandekar is a very peculiar Astrologer and Gems Expert. His clinical approach and guaranteed Musical Remedies through horoscope, distinguish him as an authentic and extraordinary personality in this field. He had developed a 9 months Music Therapy Course for pregnancy period, so as to avoid psychosomatic problems and to have a brilliant child. Actively, Dr. Bhaskar Khandekar is promoting and popularizing classical music and Performing Arts through KALAVARDHAN "Academy of Performing Arts and Events, Jabalpur. He is an Expert in "Art Therapy".

He is also Director of RAASI "Research And Advance Studies Institute", where many research scholars are doing Ph.D. under his guidance. As a musicologist, violinist and therapist Dr. Bhaskar is an eminent name of distinction and perfection making him pioneer of all his fields.[1]

He is an Events Expert and Director of Kalavardhan Event Management Services. An Image Builder and Career Launcher- A guide for establishing and improving Personal – Social and Commercial Images. He is the Chief Editor of Kalawardhan Magazine of Performing Arts News / Features in Hindi and Marathi. As well as He is a very good writer and translator in Hind-English-Marathi Language.

Achievements:

1   Sangeet Ras -Parmpara, Book - Published by Vani Prakashan Delhi. – 2001

2   Sangeet Kala Vihar Miraj By ABGM. - May 2005.

3   Sangeet Kala Vihar Miraj By ABGM. - June 2006

4   Sangeet Masik Patrika By Sangeet Karyalya Hathras UP.- July 2006.

5   Cchaya Nat Patrika By Uttar Pradesh Sangeet Natak Academy Lucknow.- September 2006.

6   Music Therapy Today Vol. 7. Issue 3, International E-Magazine - October 2006.

7   Sangeet Kala Vihar Miraj By ABGM. - Nov. 2006

8   Journal of Indian Musical Society Vadodara

9   Journal of Indian Council of Philosophical Research, New Delhi

According to him, Music has frequently been used as a therapeutic agent from the ancient times. Music is a kind of yoga system through the medium of sonorous sound, which acts upon the human organism and awakens and develops their proper functions to extent of self-realization. This is the ultimate goal of Hindu Philosophy and religion. Melody is the key-note of Indian Music. The 'Raga' is the basis of melody. Various 'Ragas', have been found to be very effective in curing many diseases.

Music helps in the treatment of actual diseases in the following manners:

1.   One obvious use of music is that of a sedative. It can replace the administration of tranquillizers, or at least reduce the dosage of tranquillizers.

2.   Music increases the metabolic activities within the human body. It accelerates the respiration, influences the internal secretion, improves the muscular activities and as such affects the "Central Nervous System" and Circulatory System of the listener and the performer.

Dr. Bhaskar's Principles of Music Therapy

Dr. Bhaskar is of opinion that: "Music Therapy is not the subject of an article only. The entire subject is now in the experimental and implementation stage and data are rapidly accumulating. And the ancient

system is gradually being transformed in to a modern science."He further says: "Since -1993, I am a practitioner of Music Therapy. After, more than five thousands patients, I have observed that - India classical 'Ragas' have been acclaimed to have healing effects. They stimulate the brain, ease tension and remove fatigue. The effect of Music Therapy may be immediate or slow, depending upon number of factors like the subject, his mental condition, environment and the type of Music, selected for having the desired effect. Music Therapy largely depends on individual needs and taste."[1] The use of Music as therapy is based on scientific and clinical approach and has to be used with great care and deep study of the nature of illness. We can call it "The study of Individual- Modality Theory". Before using music as Therapy it must be ascertained which type of music is to be used? The concept of Music Therapy is dependent on correct intonation and right use of the basic elements of music such as notes (swara) rhythm, volume, beats and piece of melody.[2] There are countless 'Ragas' of course with countless characteristic peculiarities of their own. . That is why we cannot establish a particular Rag for a particular disease. Different types of Ragas are applied in each different case. When we use term Music Therapy, we think world -wide system of therapy. Literature of Vocal part of Indian Classical Music is not sufficient in that case. I apply the formula of three 'Ps'

i. Perfect Time, - It includes duration, span, interval and time to play the music.

ii. Perfect Direction - It includes posture and conditions to listen the music.

iii. Perfect Force - It includes Tone, Timber, sound quality and volume of Meditative Music.

Remember the three categories of patients:

i.   Music Learned

ii. Music Lovers

iii. Non-Musical

The modern revival of music therapy has not yet sufficiently progressed to indicate its full utility. Several problems immediately invite further research. Under existing conditions, it would seem advisable to broaden the foundation of musical research. Not only to advance the ethical and moral rights of the human being, but also to prevent, if possible, the negative and destructive influences which may be due to ignorance of the laws governing the effects of sound and rhythm. The Indian would regard it as a sacrilege to profane his magic music, and would further insist that such profanation would destroy the healing power of the rites. It is obvious that the psychological effect of the therapeutic music would be greater if the patient understood that the scientific foundation of the procedure had been thoroughly established. He proudly says that:

> *"I take a great pleasure in introducing this contribution to the Music lovers of India. I am sure this little knowledge will prove a great help in increasing awareness for Music Therapy. Physiological, Psychological, Physical, Moral, Intellectual, and Spiritual effects of music confirm the supremacy of Indian Music."*[1]

.

Dr. Mythily Thirumalachari

Dr. Mythily Thirumalachari, a classical vocalist and music therapist, was born in an orthodox family of scholars. She hails from Tamilnadu. She started learning classical music from her child hood.[1]

She says:

"Pleasant tunes transfer good vibrations to the atmosphere. Good music brings positive vibrations in the nerves of the listener".[2]

After attained a level in rendering, till date, she is under the tutelage of world celebrity, a performing phenomenon of the century, Chevalier, Padma Vibhushan, Dr. M. Balamurali Krishna. She is a performing artist and graded by the AIR. She is a Cognitive Neuro Psychologist and Music Therapist in Apollo Hospital. Dr. T. Mythily an alumnus, of the reputed Madras University, she has submitted for her Doctorate of Science (D.sc) in her specialized area of research, Music therapy in the medical field. She was awarded Doctoral Degree for her pioneer work in the field of Psychology and Classical Music to modify the class room behavior with children in the year 1995 April. After her Masters in Psychology from the Classic Annamalai University in the year 1988, she joined the University of Madras in the year 1989 for her doctoral studies. She has more than 50 merit certificates, for proficiency in writing, and also having half-dozen Gold Medals in her pouch.[3]

She has conducted many workshops in her specialized field of interest. Many of her articles are published in leading journals. She is having more than 50 research papers to her credit. She is a linguist, proficient in Telugu, Kannada, Malayalam, Hindi, Sanskrit, two foreign languages, French and German, besides her mother tongue Tamil and English; and holds a Siromani in Sanskrit too.[1]

The GOI cultural department has awarded her JRF to do further research in her specialized field of interests for two years. She has been selected for the senior research fellow of GOI for two years 2005-2007.

She writes with both of her hands simultaneously different languages. She also conducts classes for cognitive neuropsychology. She gives research guidance to students in the higher level of learning. She also conducts many clinical studies with her students.[2]

Music Therapy as explained by Dr Mythily Thirumalachari

Music Therapy is one of the alternative forms of therapeutic treatment, it is the planned and creative use of music to attain and maintain health, well-being. Individual of any age and ability may benefit from Music Therapy program, regardless of musical skill and background. Music Therapy may address physical, psychological, emotional, cognitive and social needs with therapeutic relationships. It focuses on meeting therapeutic aims, which distinguishes it from musical entertainment or musical education.[3] Music therapy is the therapeutic application of music with proper methodologies and procedure, by trained music therapist, to restore, maintain or enhance the cognitive, socio-emotional and physical functioning of the normal/disabled persons of all ages.

Types of music Therapy:

- One is active mode of music therapy.

- The other one is passive mode of music therapy.

Music Therapy is helpful in both forms - sickness and wellness - of medical industry. In this both forms, music therapy helps to restore good health and helps to maintain the same. Active mode requires participation of the patients in the music therapy sessions, while the passive mode of music therapy requires mere involved listening. In the medical field, passive form of music therapy plays a **dominant** role in the betterment of the patients.[1]

The active mode of music therapy is useful in Pediatric areas and in few of the Neurological problems. In the **Pediatric areas**, the active mode of music therapy helps for the hyper active child to reduce the over activity in a given period of time and enhance the quality of concentration in child. With regard to speech difficulties in children this active mode of music enhances the quality of fluency in speech.

Music training also enhances the Verbal Memory improvement in children. Many of the behaviour problems in children and developmental delays and other problematic behaviours also may be attended through active mode of music therapy.[2] Music Therapy in expressive behaviour, imagination development in children, and projecting the ideas while participating etc., are all feasible in this active mode.

In the neurological areas the neurological aphasia; both the receptive and expressive aphasia may get the necessary stimulation, required to bring back the needed communication in patients. The lyrics in active music surely trigger the memory folders in the brains of patients and help to revive the same. The passive mode/form of music therapy may surely be implemented in almost in all areas of medical field as an alternative or as an adjunct or as a complement to medicine.[1]

Music therapy belongs to India

Yes. Music Therapy prevails in the universe from the dawn of the civilization, since our music is universal and have authenticity in this refined field, we can claim this form of seeking solace belongs to us. The only deficiency we have is, our forefathers do not possess the tendency or attitude to document anything which they are doing for the betterment of the society.

Effect of listening to music

Scientifically, many things are happening in our body while we are listening to the music, while we are participating in a live music session with body movements, the music which we are listening/participating many parts of the brain functions in a coordinated pattern and help to enjoy the music, if we are well versed in music. The mind has the tendency to relate or to identify things in a known pattern, accordingly come to a result/conclusion through our expressed behaviour.[2] Rather if we let the music flow into us without getting into the nuances or intricacies of the particular piece which has been provided for the therapeutic purposes, does wonder with the patients, clients and participants. Since this information and other pertaining to brain are available only through brain injured patients, few research information is available with normal healthy subjects also.

Healing effect of music

Healing effect on individuals with music is a known fact. It has centuries of claim behind it. But the quality of exposure the music with its specifications and other procedures plays a very vital role in speaking about its healing aspect.[1]

Instrumental music and music therapy

When classical music with its notes is being played through a string instrument the impact is complete. The specific notes being presented in the classical flair the impact will be good on the individuals. The music with its notes when essayed in classical format the frequency and the wavelength it emanates in the atmosphere and its impact enormous on the listeners. It helps in the quality of neuro transmitters secreted in brain and the behaviour of the individual. Music Therapy and its Essence Pleasant tunes transfer good vibrations in the atmosphere.

Music acts on our mind before being transformed into thought and feeling. Music influences the lower and higher cerebral centers of the brain. Use of Music as a therapy helps search of an Individuals personal harmony.

Music therapy is an important tool in the treatment of both physiological and psychosomatic disorders. Music Therapy stimulates good vibrations in the nerves of the listeners. Music brings about a sense of mental wellbeing in individuals. Music Therapy helps to clear the junked thought in mind, which leads to have positive frame of mind.

Music Therapy enhances the concentration level of children. Effect of music on the behaviour of individuals is enormous. Music improves the capacity of planning. Musical training helps to express refined exhibition of emotions and clarity in cognition too. Music therapy stimulates beta cell activities. Music therapy enhances quality of neural Engram.

Music therapy enhances the quality of protein releases of brain chemicals. Music therapy enhances the quality of neurotransmitters. Music therapy conditions the heart. Music therapy reduces hypertension.

Music therapy reduces unaccompanied explicit behavioural manifestations. Music therapy helps to restrain the emotional outbursts. Listening to music actually cause brain to perform better spatial reasoning. Music is part of human nature. Human brain processes music.

Effects of music on human behaviour and thought are powerful. Music enhances cognitive process. Music training and exposure increases the amount of brain that responds to musical sounds. Music during exercise produces physiological benefits. Musical interventions may reduce maternal depression and its effects on infants.[1]

Back ground music aids in developing memory. Memory recalls improves when the same music played during learning is played during recall. Music instruction is positively related to verbal memory.

Music influences the perception of art. Lyrics and tunes are processed independently in the brain. The right hemisphere is used by musicians to solve the problem. Music promotes physiological and behavioural relaxation in neonates.[2]

Music education facilitates language development and reading readiness. Direct music participation enhances the development of creativity. Art activities foster positive attitude toward studies.

Music education facilitates social development, personality adjustments and general intellectual development. Music alerts children's brain waves. Music produces a kind of pleasure which human nature cannot do without. Music is the shorthand of emotion.

Here are some relevant works by Dr. Mythily Thirumalachari on Music Therapy:

music for babies to sleep

music for Relaxation

Stop Babies crying

music for peace of mind

music to replace pain & for enhance healing

music to overcome fear & anxiety

music to overcome headache & migrane

music to enhance intellect & creativity

music to overcome sleep & relaxation

music for the heart

music for diabetes

music to enhance concentration & memory

Mrs. Rajasree Mukherjee

Rajasree Mukherjee is an Honors graduate in Zoology from Lady Brabourne College, Kolkata. She is trained in Rabindra-Sangeet under Padmasree Suchitra Mitra and ranked first class first in her Diploma examination in Rabindra Sangeet from Rabi Tirtha Institution Kolkata and second all India basis, in her Sangeet Prabhakar graduation examination at Prayag Sangeet Samiti, Allahabad. She is also a Sangeet Visharad from Pracheen Kala Kendra, Chandigarh.[1]

Settled in East Africa since 1990, Rajasree Mukherjee is one of the most popular singers there and has given numerous stage performances in Kenya, Tanzania, USA & Canada. She performed for India's President Abdul Kalam during his African visit in 2004. Through her performances she has supported several charitable organizations in East Africa.

According to her music have tremendous effects on one's physiology. This is because the roots of the auditory nerves are more widely distributed and have more connections than any other nerves in the body.[2]

1.   Sustained chords lower your pressure.

2.   Crisp, repeated chords raise your blood pressure.

3.   Music having the tempo of a normal heart beat (60-80/minute) soothes.

4. Rhythms which are slower than heart beat build suspense, since the body tends to anticipate that the music will speed up.

5. Fast rhythms raise the heart beat and excite the whole body.

Relationship between Chakras and musical notes as described by Smt. Rajasree Mukherjee.

Chakra is the Sanskrit word for wheel. They are the fast moving vortices of energy containing colors. These dynamic centers of energy make the aura brighter or dimmer depending on their activities.[1]

Each of the chakras has a characteristic frequency of vibration. It is associated with a musical note that corresponds to the frequency of its basic vibration. Color and sound can have therapeutic effect, because they can help to stimulate and balance the activity of the particular chakras. The chakras are interrelated with the endocrine glands and they should function in a balanced manner to maintain normal bodily functions.

The power of music has recently been rediscovered. The ancient Eastern philosophy that music has the power to calm the senses has now received scientific attention and acknowledgment. It is now known that music therapy activates and rejuvenates all the senses, while bringing the mind to a state of complete relaxation.

She is a leading promoter of Music Therapy[2] and has recorded several raga based meditation CDs. As an experienced Music Therapist she has used Indian Classical music to great effect in meditation techniques. She has conducted several workshops on music in Kenya widely covered by news media, Television and Radio. The Government of India has thrice honoured her by awarding grants for promotion of Indian Culture abroad.

CDs compiled by Smt. Rajasree Mukherjee

In these CDs,[1] she has generated musical compositions with the use of traditional Indian instruments such as the sarangi, sitar, and the Indian flute. Each instrument activates a different part of the brain when it strikes certain chords. This helps induce endorphins, which are the body's natural pain killers. The release of endorphins increases the sense of euphoria. These musical compositions also reduce the level of cortisol in the blood, which in turn decreases stress levels.

In order to gain the most benefit from these compositions, select a quiet place, dim the lights, sit in a relaxed posture and keep your back straight. You can either choose to close your eyes or keep them half open. Switch on the music, slowly empty your mind of all thoughts and

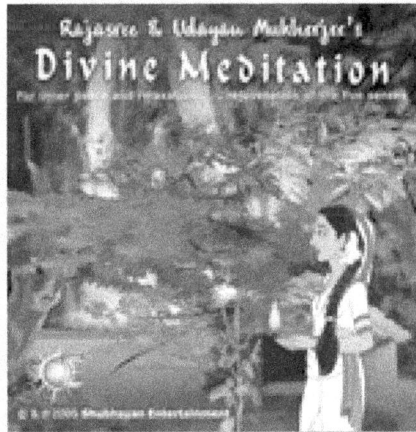

loosen the muscles of your body. All kinds of thoughts will rush through your mind, let them pass without analysing or acting upon them until your mind is quiet.

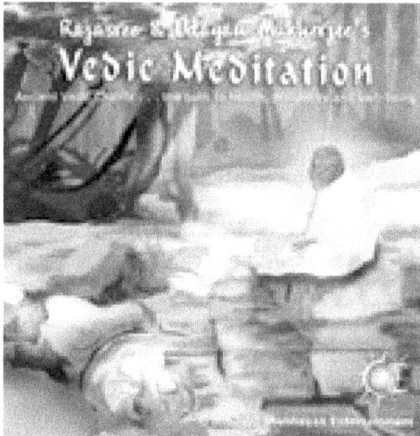

Let your mind and body respond instinctively to the music without any pre-conceived ideas of the effect of the music on your body. Relax and let the music envelop you. Feel the music cleansing your mind and body, spreading a warm glow throughout every cell of your body, and diminishing discomfort and stress.

MUSIC THERAPY ROUND THE GLOBE

After having a glance at the research done on music therapy in India, Now, we will cover some authors and researchers from round the globe to have an idea about their methods and perceptions on Music therapy which is as followed:

John M. Ortiz – United states of America

John M. Ortiz, Ph.D. (1952-2012), was the founder and director of The Institute of Applied Psycho musicology (SM). He was a licensed psychologist, educator, consultant, author, musician, certified clinical hypnotist and psycho educational trainer. Listed in the National Register of Health Service Providers in Psychology, his professional affiliations included the American Counselling Association, American Music Therapy Association, American School Counsellor Association, and Association for Humanistic Psychology. He served on the editorial board of the American Counselling Association's Journal of Counselling and Development between 1996-1998. His international lectures on Sound Psychology were based on his books published by Samuel Weiser, Inc., 1997, and was published by Beyond Words, Pub; Hillsboro, Oregon, December, 1999.[1]

Sound Psychology Research

Dr. Ortiz began researching the effects of combining traditional psychological approaches with music and sound in the mid 1970's while working at a number of mental health facilities as counsellor, therapist and vocational evaluator. His doctoral dissertation, "The Facilitating Effects of

Soothing Background Music on an Initial Counselling Session" (Penn State University, 1991), along with other research conducted while at Penn State University in the late 1980's, helped to strongly support and expand the base of some of the Sound Psychology ideas that have led to his popular books and CD series.

Some of the works done by Dr. John M. Ortiz[1]

The Tao of Music : Sound Psychology

Dr. Ortiz has focused on this basic impulse and created an effective systematic way to deal with life's vagaries, whether they're long-term problems or momentary difficulties. He uses carefully selected songs and melodies, reflective of specific emotional states, that we can each use to progress from identifying our pain to healing it.

Designed as an introduction to Sound Psychology™, The Tao of Music: Sound Psychology combines music and sound, basic psychological principles, and Eastern philosophy in a "reader friendly," practical format, making it accessible to laypersons as well as health practitioners. Through a wealth of inspirational case stories, simple exercises and creative techniques, this holistic, extensively researched resource provides hundreds of recommended "Musical Menus" to assist readers in "composing" their own complementary programs for healing, prevention and wellness.

The Soothing Pulse

The Soothing Pulse; A companion to the popular book The Tao of Music: Sound Psychology, consists of a progressive relaxation exercise that combines various techniques such as drones (calming, ongoing sounds), a hemispheric synchronization pulse ("hemi-sync"), and a progressive relaxation script that escorts the listener into a deep relaxation or meditation while following a descending (around 80 to 54 beats per minute) tempo.

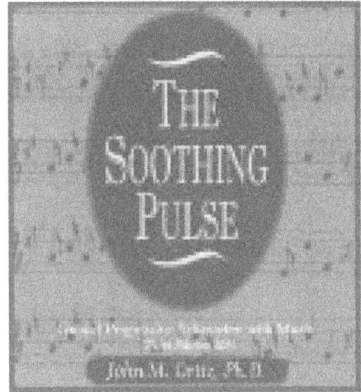

The entrainment technique used in the CD was developed throughout years of research and experimentation that were part of Dr. Ortiz's graduate studies and, later, doctoral dissertation at Penn State University.[1]

Based on the technique of Pulse Entrainment, The Soothing Pulse is designed to synchronize, and then gradually slow down our internal pulses and rhythms leading to a state of natural mind-body relaxation.

The progressive relaxation sequence introduced in this quieting exercise accomplishes this by using a combination of Applied Psycho-musicology techniques intended to help us achieve a state of deep, restful meditation.

Nurturing Your Child With Music:

This wonderful book will help parents learn how to use music and sound to enrich their children's lives. The book's goal is to raise Sound Awareness and to assist parents in creating family harmony and strengthening lifelong bonds.[1]

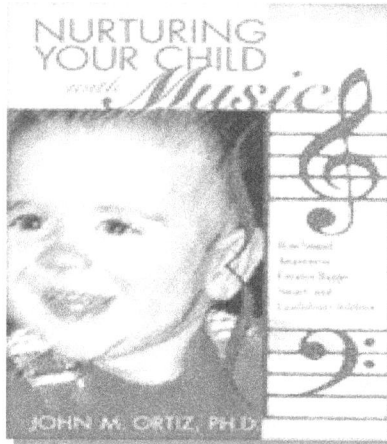

Nurturing Your Child with Music offers sound ideas to assist young children in getting to sleep, relaxation, stimulation, enhancing creativity and coordination and developing musical interest. It also introduces many musical games and activities to bring families together.

The chapters are designed to stand on their own so if a child won't do his chores, skip right to chapter eleven, "With a Little Help from My Kids," for music to inspire tooth-brushing and putting toys away (use made-up lyrics or use the ones provided) and motivate the child to help around the house. Don't despair about listening to another "Chipmunks" volume. Ortiz emphasizes that the menus are just suggestions. If parents like a particular

---

1. http://www.soundpsych.com/nycm_bk.html

type of music, they should go ahead and play it for the children, too. Different types of music suit different needs.[1]

Felicity Baker & Jeanette Tamplin

Associate Professor Felicity Baker is an Australia Research Council Future Fellow (2011-2015) in the area of music therapy and working on a study that aims to build a therapeutic model of song-writing across the lifespan.[2] She is Founding Director of the International Research Network of Therapeutic Song-writing which has 32 members from 12 countries. Her clinical and research expertise are predominantly in neuro-rehabilitation with a special interest in communication rehabilitation and facilitating emotional adjustment to a changed identity via various music therapy methods. Felicity is National President of The Australian Music Therapy Association, the national peak body for the discipline, and former editor of The Australian Journal of Music Therapy. She holds editorial board membership on The Journal of Music Therapy and the Nordic Journal of Music Therapy and has taught on international music therapy programs in Taiwan, USA, Germany, Denmark, Norway, and the United Kingdom. Felicity was awarded a University of Queensland Foundation Excellence in Research Award (2008), an Australian Learning and Teaching Council Citation Award (2009), and an ADC Australian Leadership Award (2011). Felicity has published widely with over 70 publications and is best known for her authored and edited

texts: Music Therapy in Neuro-rehabilitation: A Clinician's Manual. Jessica Kingsley Publishers (2006 with Jeanette Tamplin), Song Writing Methods, Techniques and Clinical Applications for Music Therapy Clinicians, Educators and Student (2005, with Tony Wigram), and Voice-work in Music Therapy: Research and Practice (2011, with Sylka Uhlig).[1]

Work done by Felicity Baker

Music Therapy Methods in Neurorehabilitation: A Clinician's Manual

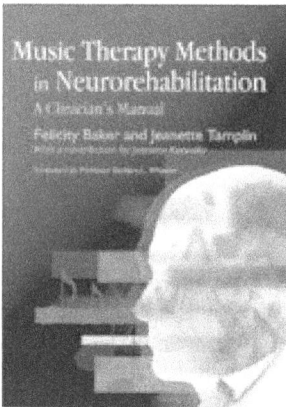

Felicity Baker and Jeanette Tamplin combine research findings with their own clinical experience and present step-by-step instructions and guidelines on how to implement music therapy techniques for a range of therapeutic needs.

Photographs clearly illustrate interventions for physical rehabilitation, for example through the use of musical instruments to encourage targeted movement.[2]

The chapter on cognitive rehabilitation includes resources and lists suitable songs for use in immediate memory or abstract thinking tasks, among others. In her chapter on paediatric patients, Jeanette Kennelly demonstrates how procedures can be adapted for working clinically with children. A comprehensive list of terminology commonly used in neurological rehabilitation is also included.

_____

Dr. Kenneth Bruscia – *Philadelphia USA*

(Professor Emeritus of Music Therapy)

Dr. Bruscia has professional certifications in music therapy (MT-BC), Guided Imagery and Music (FAMI), and mandala assessment, and has several years of clinical experience with diverse clientele, including individuals with intellectual disability, psychiatric disorders, cancer, AIDS, psychoneuroses, PTSD, and the elderly. Previously on the piano faculty of Duquesne University and music therapy faculty at New York University[1], he came to Temple in 1974 where he founded the bachelor's, Master's, and PhD degrees in music therapy. The PhD degree is the first true doctoral degree in music therapy in the USA. Dr. Bruscia has served as Music Therapy Program Coordinator, PhD Coordinator, Director of Graduate Studies in Music and Dance, and member/chair of several college and university committees.

He has received the Lind-back Award for Teaching, The Temple University Great Teacher Award, the Temple University Research Award, and the AMTA Research and Publication Awards. He has served as President of the American Association for Music Therapy, Chair of the National Coalition of Arts Therapies, and an officer on numerous organizational committees, for which he has received three awards for service to the profession.[2] He has served on the editorial boards of four major journals (Music Therapy, Music Therapy Perspectives, Arts in Psychotherapy, Journal of Music Therapy), and founded the International Newsletter of

Music Therapy. Since 1978, he has given 205 lectures and workshops around the world. His books are frequently used as texts, and have been translated into several languages; his writings are widely cited throughout the music therapy literature.

His current research interests include:

- Phenomenological and heuristic methods of music analysis;

- Narrative methods of researching client experiences;

- Heuristic methods of studying therapist experiences;

- Projective methods of clinical assessment;

- The development of research paradigms for music psychotherapy, particularly Guided Imagery and Music; and

- Development of music therapy theory; Quantitative efficacy research[1]

Jonathan Goldman

Jonathan Goldman, M.A. is an international authority on sound healing and a pioneer in the field of harmonics. He is author of Healing Sounds, Shifting Frequencies, The Lost Chord, the best selling The 7 Secrets Of Sound Healing, Chakra Frequencies (co-authored with his wife Andi), and his latest The Divine Name, winner of the 2011 Visionary Award for "Best Alternative Health Book".[2]

Jonathan is director of the Sound Healers Association and president of Spirit Music, Inc. in Boulder, Colorado. A Grammy nominee, he has created numerous best selling, award winning recordings including "THE DIVINE NAME" (with Gregg Braden), "REIKI CHANTS", "FREQUENCIES: Sounds of Healing", THE LOST CHORD", "2012: ASCENSION HARMONICS" and "CHAKRA CHANTS", double winner of Visionary Awards for "Best Healing-Meditation Album" and "Album of the Year". Jonathan is a lecturing member of the International Society for Music Medicine. He has dedicated his life to the path of service, helping awaken and empower others with the ability of sound to heal and transform.

In spring 2011, Jonathan was named as one of Watkin's Reviews "100 Most Spiritually Influential People on the Planet." In 2011, Jonathan was inducted into the Massage Therapy's Hall of Fame. He presents HEALING SOUNDS lectures, workshops and seminars worldwide.[1]

Jonathan is the director of the Sound Healers Association; the original organization dedicated to the education and awareness of sound and music for healing. He is also president of Spirit Music, which produces music for meditation, relaxation and self-transformation. Jonathan has created numerous cutting edge, best selling recordings including: "Chakra Chants" won the 1999 Visionary Awards for "Best Healing-Meditation Album" and "Album of the Year", "2012: Ascension Harmonics" winner of the Visionary Award for "Best Healing-Meditation" in 2010. Other highly acclaimed award winning albums: "The Lost Chord", "The Divine Name" (co-created with Gregg Braden), "Reiki Chants", "ChakraDance", "Ultimate Om", "Holy Harmony", "Crystal Bowls Chakra Chants". His latest album include: "2013: Ecstatic Sonics", "Chakra/Brainwave Harmonizer" and

"Cosmic Hum". His collaboration with Tibetan Chant Master Lama Tashi "Tibetan Master Chants" was been nominated for a 2006 Grammy Award for "Best Traditional World Music". His overtone chanting is heard on Kitaro's 2001 Grammy Award winning album.[1]

Jonathan has written numerous articles on the therapeutic and transformational uses of sound and music, which have appeared in many national publications. He has also contributed chapters and interviews to many books, including: MUSIC MEDICINE, SONIC ALCHEMY, MUSIC: PHYSICIAN FOR TIMES TO COME and HEALING SPIRITS. Jonathan's work has been cited in many books, including Julia Cameron's VEIN OF GOLD. The McGraw-Hill college text, MUSIC IN OUR WORLD, has a chapter on Jonathan's recording of "Dolphin Dreams". In DA VINCI DECODED, Jonathan's CD "Chakra Chants" is listed as the #1 Selection on the "Top Ten Spiritual Playlist".

An internationally acknowledge Master Teacher, Jonathan facilitates Healing Sounds Seminars at universities, hospitals, holistic health centers and expos throughout the United States and Europe. He has appeared on national television and radio, including Art Bell's "Coast to Coast AM" and has been featured in national periodicals including "USA Today" and "The New York Times". His annual Healing Sounds Intensive attracts participants from throughout the world.[2]

Mr. Jonathan is of opinion that·

"For most people who believe that music healing and sound healing are the same, the only option they're willing to try is the experience of listening to a recording of therapeutic music. They believe that's all they're capable

---

of as non-musicians. Listening to music can, of course, be extremely healing. But at the beginning of our presentations, I frame the concept of Sound Healing saying: "We are not talking about getting up and singing in front of an audience. That's entertainment. And it can be very healing. But what we are talking about is a phenomenon of physics called "entrainment", in which the vibrations of objects literally shift their frequencies." That is sound healing![1]

As per him "Music can create powerful shifts and changes. But, on a more accessible level, so can the toning of an elongated vowel such as an "Ah". Which everyone can do! Even 5 minutes of making a simple humming sound has extraordinary therapeutic benefits." Here are just some of the many different physiological benefits that can be achieved through self-created sound:

- Increased oxygen in the cells
- Lowered blood pressure and heart rate
- Increased levels of melatonin—to enhance sleep and reduce depression
- Reduced levels of stress related hormones
- Release of endorphins—self-created opiates that work as "natural pain relievers"
- Release of Nitric Oxide—the "molecule of the year" and a vascular dilator
- Release of Oxytocin—the trust hormone

He emphasizes, that these extraordinary benefits are not being generated through use of any sort of expensive device or an instrument that needs lots of practice. It's not even necessary to have any special vocal ability vocal ability or be trained singer in order to experience powerful results. These various benefits occur simply through making self-created sounds that anyone can manifest.

Mr. Jonathan further states: "I created this delineation between sound and music to hopefully remove the common first assumption that they are the same. I hope that this thoughtform will serve to help open the world of sound healing up to as many people as possible. The highest goal is to remove any perceived barrier of an "us and them" mentality. If those of us teaching sound healing encourage this awareness, then sound healing becomes inclusive instead of exclusive (which often occurs when it is confused with music healing). From my perspective, we can all very easily learn to use our voice (among other things) as an extraordinary instrument of sound healing.[1]

Here are some of the books authored by Mr. Jonathan:[2]

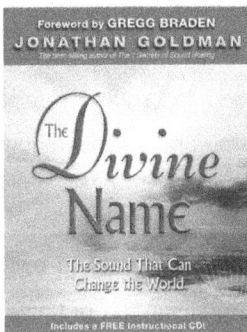

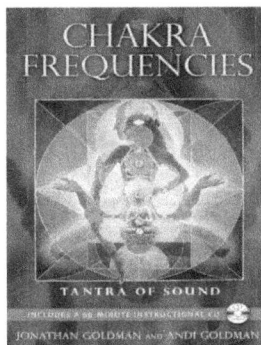

Here are some CDsby Mr. Jonathan on sound and Music therapy:[1]

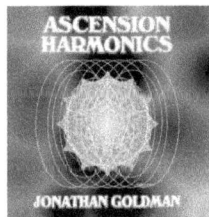

When we talk about Music therapy on a global level then it is really hard to justice to this vast topic in some limited pages. Still, an effort is always worth having if we are able to quote some important information related to the topic. And, it follows:

Research has shown that in many parts of Africa during male and female circumcision, bone setting, or traditional surgery and bloodletting, lyrical music related to endurance has been used to reduce anticipated pain, therapeutically. In 1999, the first program for music therapy in Africa opened in Pretoria, South Africa.[1]

Research has shown that in Tanzania patients can receive palliative care for life-threatening illnesses directly after the diagnosis of these illnesses. This is different from many Western countries, because they reserve palliative care for patients who have an incurable illness. Music is also viewed differently between Africa and Western countries. In Western countries and a majority of other countries throughout the world, music is traditionally seen as entertainment whereas in many African cultures, music is used in recounting stories, celebrating life events, or sending messages.[2]

In Australia in 1949, music therapy (not clinical music therapy as understood today) was started through concerts organized by the Australian Red Cross along with a Red Cross Music Therapy Committee. The key Australian body, AMTA, the Australian Music Therapy Association, was founded in 1975.[3]

Music therapy has existed in its current form in the United States since 1944 when the first undergraduate degree program in the world was begun at Michigan State University and the first graduate degree program was established at the University of Kansas. The American Music Therapy Association (AMTA) was founded in 1998 as a merger between the National Association for Music Therapy (NAMT, founded in 1950) and the

American Association for Music Therapy (AAMT, founded in 1971). Numerous other national organizations exist, such as the Institute for Music and Neurologic Function, Nordoff Robbin's Center for Music Therapy, and the Association for Music and Imagery. Music therapists use ideas from different disciplines such as speech and language, physical therapy, medicine, nursing, and education.[1]

After the personal researches which we have mentioned and discussed here, formal research degrees come on the mind. There are many institutions and organizations which hold the criteria up and support the professional training of music therapy and also promotes research programmes on the same.

A music therapy degree candidate can earn an undergraduate, master's or doctoral degree in music therapy. Many AMTA approved programs offer equivalency and certificate degrees in music therapy for students that have completed a degree in a related field. Some practicing music therapists have held PhDs in fields other than, but usually related to, music therapy. Recently, Temple University established a PhD program in music therapy. A music therapist typically incorporates music therapy techniques with broader clinical practices such as psychotherapy, rehabilitation, and other practices depending on client needs. Music therapy services rendered within the context of a social service, educational, or health care agency are often reimbursable by insurance and sources of funding for individuals with certain needs. Music therapy services have been identified as reimbursable under Medicaid, Medicare, private insurance plans and federal and state government programs.[2]

A degree in music therapy requires proficiency in guitar, piano, voice, music theory, music history, reading music, improvisation, as well as varying levels of skill in assessment, documentation, and other counseling and health care skills depending on the focus of the particular university's program. A music therapist may hold the designations CMT (Certified Music Therapist), ACMT (Advanced Certified Music Therapist), or RMT (Registered Music Therapist) – credentials previously conferred by the former national organizations AAMT and NAMT; these credentials remain in force through 2020 and have not been available since 1998. The current credential available is MT-BC. To become board certified, a music therapist must complete a music therapy degree from an accredited AMTA program at a college or university, successfully complete a music therapy internship, and pass the Board Certification Examination in Music Therapy, administered through The Certification Board for Music Therapists .To maintain the credential, either 100 units of continuing education must be completed every five years, or the board exam must be retaken near the end of the five-year cycle. The units claimed for credit fall under the purview of The Certification Board for Music Therapists. North Dakota, Nevada and Georgia have established licenses for music therapists. In the State of New York, the License for Creative Arts Therapies (LCAT) incorporates the music therapy credentials within their licensure.[1]

In United Kingdom live music was used in hospitals after both World Wars as part of the treatment program for recovering soldiers. Clinical music therapy in Britain as it is understood today was pioneered in the 1960s and 1970s by French cellist Juliette Alvin whose influence on the current generation of British music therapy lecturers remains strong. Mary Priestley, one of Juliette Alvin's students, created "analytical music therapy". The Nordoff Robbin's approach to music therapy developed from the work of Paul Nordoff and Clive Robbins in the 1950/60s.[1]

Practitioners are registered with the Health Professions Council and, starting from 2007 new registrants must normally hold a master's degree in music therapy. There are master's level programs in music therapy in Manchester, Bristol, Cambridge, South Wales, Edinburgh and London, and there are therapists throughout the UK. The professional body in the UK is the British Association for Music Therapy. In 2002, the World Congress of Music Therapy, coordinated and promoted by the World Federation of Music Therapy, was held in Oxford on the theme of Dialogue and Debate. In November 2006, Dr. Michael J. Crawford and his colleagues again found that music therapy helped the outcomes of schizophrenic patients.[2]

Be it in India or round the globe, music has played its important therapeutic role in human life. Techniques and implementation could differ but the mission in same.

CHAPTER – 6

The Cultural Uniqueness of Music Therapy: A mix of Eastern and a Western Voice.

CHAPTER 6

THE CULTURAL UNIQUENESS OF MUSIC THERAPY: A MIX OF EASTERN AND A WESTERN VOICE

Eastern Voice: - All civilizations in the ancient world, like those of East, have established and developed their musical art on the basis of extremely precise observations of the effect of sound phenomena and rations on human sensitivity, thought and behavior. Music here has always aimed at causing certain reactions, developing certain tendencies and aptitudes, and communicating ideas and feelings. In the Shaivite world, music became an essential part of ritual and developed as a refined art, the principal instrument of a certain form of spiritual life. Siva is represented as the creator of musical art, and his devotees the *bhaktas* used model thought and its developments as a mean of inner concentration and perception of the super natural. All "Scholarly" music in India, pursues this musical ideal that shapes the inner man, harmonizing and improving him, drawing him towards an inner pursuit that Insulates him from material worries.

India is known for its rich cultural heritage and traditions. If music therapy in India is to be understood one has to understand the science and sound of music which was studied so intricately and understood so deeply in ancient India. Additionally there is the country's tantric religious philosophy with its higher levels of understanding of the expansion of different levels of human consciousness. Indian music therapy is strongly influenced by such ancient sacred and musical practices as Vedic Recitals, Raga Chikitsa, Nada Yoga and Nadopasana and traditional alternative healing systems like Yoga and Ayurveda. All these approaches integrate with music, spirituality adding uniqueness to the practice of music therapy, making it a holistic approach to the enhancement of wellness and health in the art of living.

Western Voice:-Western music appears to be unique in that it has no defined goal, basing its theory on physical or acoustic details of sounds that are moreover very approximate, rather than on their potential as a vehicle for some communicable content.

The uniqueness of music therapy practice lies in the multiple styles adopted by different practitioners across the globe depending on the colorful ethnic fabric of the region where it is practiced. This is unlike other health care approaches which are standardized. The flexibility in balancing broader aspects like life style, philosophical orientation, the musical traditions and cultural heritage of a specific region and integrating them in clinical practice drives us constantly to improve and develop the practice.

As, we have already discussed the different point of views of eastern and western people on Music therapy, Now, we will get to know about the logical background of applying music therapy and about the benefits from music therapy according to both the point of views, which are as followed:

Dr. John M. Ortiz said: "Music is God's way of coloring sound!"[1]He further mentions:

> *"Bottom line: it doesn't matter "how" or "why." Singing, chanting, toning, humming, whistling, all help to release endorphins, which helps us to feel better!"*

An Interview with Mr. Aurelio is of real importance from the point of view of the heading which we have taken for this chapter.

Mr. Aurelio, Director of Svaram Musical Instruments Research Station, Director and Trustee, Mohanam Cultural Centre situated at Auroville Community, Pondicherry, India is a musician/composer, sound healer, music therapist and a cultural activist. Although educated in Austria in linguistics and music ethnology, he has settled in a community in Auroville and dedicated his life to a social cause through his work in music and sound. Svaram is one of the few places on the Indian subcontinent experimenting in the field of creating of new musical instruments that should be accessible to everybody, independent of talent or predisposition, directly bringing the joy of music into one's hands and heart.

Mr. Aurelio was asked in an Interview that: ***"Where do western and eastern philosophies meet or do they meet at all in music therapy practice?"***

And, his reply was: *"Philosophically east or west always meant to befriend with the truth, to find out more about the origin, reason and aim of our life. Whereas in the West with its preoccupation with rational thinking the methods were more speculative and reductionist and pedagogic, the East relied more on contemplative experience, intuition and direct transmission. So this offers now a marvelous opportunity for a synthesis and integrative approach, bringing together the diverse strains of human explorations into the nature and expression of our highest ideals of love, beauty, knowledge and power. With the emergence of a new paradigm for a global civilization it becomes redundant to emphasize or stress the dualities and seems more important to discover and utilize the wisdom and achievements of any tradition. For music therapy this shall mean openness to the rich traditions of healing through sound and music from all over the globe and at the same time work on research and methodologies according to the defined scientific parameters. The question for the future is probably not so much one of different philosophies but rather the finding, defining and utilization of a pragmatic science of an Integral Psychology."[1]*

Mr. Aurelio further adds:

"For the field of music therapy in India that could bring a vast array of explorations and research into its rich artistic, medical and spiritual heritage, fresh and scientifically based experimentation and inspired and creative applications of one of the richest and most complex music systems of humanity."[2]

He was further asked: ***"What do you think Indian music therapists can do?"***

Aurelio: *"Here again it is not anymore a question of left or right, east or west, either or, but rather if we manage as contemporary conscious humans to take the leap into an understanding or should we better say over-view of our present situation and evolutionary crises on all levels of our planetary existence. We can take responsibility to grow in wisdom and compassion to heal ourselves and fellow sentient beings and co-create a more harmonious life in resonance with truly wholesome principles and universal values. The music therapist in India can take advantage of the deep wisdom traditions and practices of this special culture; be familiar with Ayurvedic principles and Yoga psychology and its diverse branches like Nada, Svara and Nidra Yoga, tantric, occult and indigenous practices; be deeply experienced in the classical Indian music, while also*

---

comprehending other systems and at the same time be trained and satisfy academic and scientific methodologies. In this way a really unique curriculum for trainings and courses could be developed which would also draw interest and participation from the international field."[1]

And then he was asked: ***"Have you ever thought that the western approaches of musical therapy interfered with the culture, life style and the philosophic orientation of this country (India)?"***

Aurelio: *"We are actually quite fortunate within the practice of music therapy, with its renaissance either from the ancient wisdom tradition or from a postmodern holistic world view, that we can approach our subject from a more integral perspective. Even in the pure clinical work we work with the understanding of the whole phenomena of the client and not with isolated symptomatic treatments. Even if there might be pure physical phenomena and the possibility of treatments through mere vibrations and selected frequencies, the strength and future significance of music therapy is its possible integration of the physical, the emotional, vital field, the conceptions, thinking sphere and the spiritual dimension of our being, as exemplified in the Ayurvedic system. Be it with scientific methods, shamanic techniques, psychotherapeutic approaches or mystic means, it is in the perception and understanding of the fullness of our existence that we will have the capacity to harmonize discords and heal and bring the fragmentation and isolation into the natural symphonic state of our cosmic existence, individually, in the collective and the world. The global re-emergence of music and sound therapies is a clear indication of natures-*

human and planetary need to realign to a deeper harmony and order of the cosmos. What a delight and responsibility to be instrumental in that work!"[1]

The interview further went on asking with: ***Can you please tell us what exactly attracted you to settle down in Auroville community in India as a sound healer and a cultural activist even though you have a very strong background in western music, having been educated and trained in Austria?***

Aurelio: In many of my studies in the west on the healing potential and metaphysics of sound I found constant referrals to the Indian tradition and its deep knowledge and wisdom of sound. What attracted me was the contemplative and experiential approach, and I had a strong need to dive deeper into that unknown ocean of sound, to fathom its magic, discover its mystery, scrutinize the concepts and facts, so that through my own experience I would understand directly and be able to apply the healing power of sound on myself and others. Of course it became clear through many contacts, studies and practices that this is a life long journey, and that as in a true vidya, a deep knowledge and science of life - the secrets reveal themselves only according to inner capacity, dedication and discipline and the right timing.

A question again was put up: ***What do you think about the status of music therapy in India? Do you find anything different?***

Aurelio: It is interesting that in spite of many myths and legends about the magic of music we don't find very many direct references in the scriptures or contemporary music practice about healing with sound or music therapy. As is so typical in many other areas of the Indian tradition, much is shrouded in mystery of the sacrosanct past and there is also a strain of resistance of approaching the subject too directly and rationally. So I have some quite interesting anecdotes of encounters with musicians, nadayogis, occultists, spiritual researchers and scientists and it has been a long, adventurous journey to come to a kind of comprehensive view on the subject. As such there is not yet an established practice of Indian music therapy but, as in its religion and philosophy, a multifarious array of approaches and attitudes ranging from the primal sound magic of the tribal cultures, through the deep spiritual sound healing techniques of some mystery schools, to international acclaimed research on music and life force. Through all these shines the underlying principle of the creative, sustaining and transformative power of sound as an expression of the origin, interrelatedness and oneness of our existence. India could make through its holistic view and wisdom, essential and important contributions to the field of music therapy, as for example the total approach of Ayurveda as a science of life already contributes substantially to our understanding of individual, social and environmental health. One of the most important treatises on music, whose author hailed from a family of medical practitioners, starts its exposition of musical axioms, written in verse, with a whole cosmology and embryology of our human becoming and defines the ultimate role of music as being to lead us out of any bondage and suffering to the highest human potential of liberation and enlightenment.[1]

The next question was: **Though a music composer, you integrate music therapy in all your activities in Svaram. How do you find**

---

integrating your western musical background into a typical cultural and traditional eastern setting?

Aurelio: *It became so apparent in the grass roots work that one cannot separate the individual's state of health from his social upbringing, conditionings and present circumstances. The facts of big households and joint families and kinship patterns and clan and caste structures have to be understood and integrated for a wholesome harmonization to occur. It proved also extremely rewarding to work on instrument building directly, with the unemployed youth, to get hands-on with the craft work as this brought us plenty of learning opportunities about diverse materials and their sound properties, about acoustic principles, and the classifications and symbolism of the different instrument classes and genres of traditional and contemporary music. My western education and rational training was very helpful to discern, analyze, bring in context, develop step by step methodologies, overview and strategize our work and development process. I believe firmly that we are globally at a stage where we can benefit from all different approaches and traditions and discover afresh and develop a synthesis of the golden means and centre which brings together the right and left hemispheres, the eastern and western approaches, and the micro and macro views of our human perspective and world divide and prepare us for the next evolutionary step in this civilization of change. Music in the Indian tradition has been seen and heard as a powerful agent, catalyst, and bridge between the layers and spheres of the cosmos and therefore can fulfill a prime function towards a healing and emerging integral consciousness.*

And the next question was: **"What would be your view on the future of music therapy in India, and the possible contribution of your project work?"**

Aurelio:"_Many of the international researchers and spiritual seekers from abroad living in India share the perception that this culture has something very valuable and essential to contribute towards a functioning and healthier future of our global civilization. This ancient tradition speaks about the Sanathana Dharma, a universal truth, law, way an expression of our deepest human longings and highest ideals of perfection. Music has always held the highest place amongst the arts, was sacred and revered as a gift from and a gateway to higher realms of existence. It was seen as a means for salvation. Many people in the world have experienced in the last decades the uplifting and soothing and soulful qualities of Indian classical music, and the vitality and charm of its folk forms. It will be a rewarding task to uncover and recreate, define and formulate a specific and yet organic system and discipline of Indian music therapy.[1] At this moment there are some pioneering initiatives preparing the ground and we hope that our work with our instrument building and research in sound healing modalities will open a vaster field of interest, communication and international collaborations._

The ever present drone of the Indian sound's cape is inviting for a free melodic and rhythmic flow. Healing spaces open meaningfully and time reveals the play of our precious life here on earth!"

At last, a very sensitive and the most important question related to our topic, was answered very beautifully by Mr. Aurelio and the question was: **"Do you do both sound healing and music therapy? If yes, is your sound healing in tune with the eastern culture and music therapy to the western?"**

Aurelio: *"I welcome the emergence of differentiation of the means and components of music therapy. What would be a clear distinction between sound healing and music therapy? Is it that the east placed more emphasis on the inner dimensions of sound and that the west explored more its structural manifestation, that the east approached healing through the essence and aim of our life, that the west was preoccupied with problem solving and therapeutic techniques? If we take it again from an integral point of view then all the factors work together in a successful treatment and process of positive change. Music is a total phenomenon and even if it and its impact can be analyzed and taken apart into its purely material, vibrations, sound components on one side and its structural, aesthetic, conception part on the other, and that we would say that one works purely on the physical and the other on the emotional and mental, if we don't account for all the aspects of the intricate process and relationship, the social, cultural and environmental conventions, conditionings and circumstances, then again we fall back into the separatist attitude of our predominant logical and therefore limited view.*

Music therapy will play a growing role in the future healing arts if it takes and incorporates the premises of its prime means: music, which is a unique and rare wholesome expression of human life exemplifying the full potential of our nature and connecting us with a world of harmony and perfection.[1] That is why it is crucial for music therapy and its proponents to approach this precious gift for our well-being and healing through a renaissance of the ancient wisdom and now again newly emerging paradigm of integrality and wholeness.

In that way, yes, we are looking for a synthesis, and have the amazing benefit, chance and tool with music therapy to work and live from and through the spirit of harmony of this higher or deeper, transcendent or immanent dimension of our existence, which is opening and communicating to us through the realm of music.[1]

On the basis of this interview with Mr. Aurelio, a fact comes in front of our eyes that he believes in Universal Music therapy and gives both the voices; Eastern & Western.

Here, it won't be an exaggeration if we quote one of his statements once again which is quite comprehensive to his approach:

> *"It is crucial for music therapy and its proponents to approach this precious gift for our well-being and healing through a renaissance of the ancient wisdom and now again newly emerging paradigm of integrality and wholeness."*

In the above statement, he refers to the **Indian ancient system as the ancient wisdom and finds a base in it**; Whereas, Western system as a newly emerging paradigm of integrality and wholeness.

There are many organizations worldwide, which are dedicated to developing and promoting music therapy throughout the world as an art and science. They also support the global development of educational programs, clinical practice, and research to demonstrate the contributions of music therapy to humanity.

They also bring the opportunity to practice music therapy and the benefits of music therapy interventions to people throughout the world with the values like safe refuge, well-being, dignity, and education as the fundamental human rights. These organizations believe in the musical power which can heal and promote well-being. They also advocate for the use of music to promote equity, social justice, and peaceful resolution. And, support a global music therapy network that includes all cultural and ethnic backgrounds – age, religion, social status, sexual orientation, gender, indigenous heritage, and disability encouraging open, on-going communication as the foundation of learning and growth for the profession of a music therapist.

At the end of this chapter some quotes by the worldwide philosophers will be mentioned. The quotes are talking about the role of music in building the individual and the society as a whole; the spiritual powers of music and the social uses of music. In short, music being therapeutic beyond the boundaries but taking care of the global community.

The quotes are as followed:

> *"Any song — whether it is a love-song or otherwise — if one's whole soul is in that song, one attains salvation, one has nothing else to do. They say it leads to the same goal as meditation."*[1]

Swami Vivekananda

> *"Music is a higher revelation than all wisdom and philosophy."*[2]

Ludwig van Beethoven

> *"Music is the movement of sound to reach the soul for the education of its virtue."*[3]

Plato

_____

"Music is the purest form of art, therefore true poets, they who are seers, seek to express the universe in terms of music... The singer has everything within him. The notes come out from his very life. They are not materials gathered from outside."[1]

Rabindranath Tagore quotes

"Music directly imitates the passions or states of the soul, when one listens to music that imitates a certain passion, he becomes imbued withthe same passion; and if over a long time he habitually listens to music that rouses ignoble passions, his whole character will be shaped to an ignoble form."[2]

Aristotle

Musical training is a more potent instrument than any other, because rhythm and harmony find their way into the inward places of the soul, on which they mightily fasten, imparting grace, and making the soul of him who is rightly educated graceful, or of him who is ill-educated ungraceful.[3]

Socrates

CONCLUSION

CONCLUSION

Indian music literature is very old. It dates back to Vedic period. References to music are found in the Vedas, Upnishad, Puranas and other religious books e.g. Ramayana, Mahabharata. Music material is also available in Buddhist and Jain religious books. With passage of time more and more books were written, all these are of utmost for studying history of music. I have made a sincere effort to cover the significant history of Indian Music in this Research work, from the origin to the development of Indian Music. How Indian Music used to be thought of and how it used to create a difference in the life of people in remote past.

It is said that a country in which there is no musical education is far behind in the scale of civilization. Its people are selfish and inhospitable, and wanting in that trait of character which makes them to love and be loved by others. Music is sympathy and it is desirable that the prince as well as the peasant should be musical. That country in which the ruler is musical will be happy, contented and prosperous, for he rules not by force of his sceptre but by his heart, which finds a ready response in every subject.

In this research work I have quoted many references to prove the role of Indian Music as a therapeutic healer for one and for all. Meditation based on 'Nada', worshipping through music based on 'Nadopasana'; Chikitsa based on 'Ragas', the recitation of Indian Music based on 'Chanting' and 'Toning'; the Important role of Tala in One's Life; Importance of sound (Musical Voice) and its association with prayer , these are the key points which have been discussed in this research work.

Prof. Anjali Mittal has quoted some very deep lines in one of her books:

"What do we mean by words like art, expression, feeling, creation, rasa or aesthetic experience? This is indeed a very important question which is discussed by philosophical aesthetics today. Nor is this question any way artificial. For the fact indeed is that what these words mean in relation to art is, in many cases, different from what they mean in daily conversation. Take, to begin with, the word art. It is true that even in everyday conversation this word is used in three distinct senses: art as an object of art, art as a distinct kind of activity, and art as signifying all objects of a particular kind. But, everyday talk does not try to think out how art, as an object of art, differs from the objects that we deal with in daily life. Art is significant primarily because it opens up our contemplation, a whole new world of feelings, form and images; which is quite independent of the considerations of truth, reality and utility.[1]"

On the basis of this deep statement by Prof. Anjali Mittal, in relation to the therapy through Music after studying what Music therapy is, paying attention to the constitution of music therapy- beyond the boundaries, and analyzing the role of music therapy in the healing process of mankind; we can say if this art of Indian music will be used with truth and in reality then it can be of great utility. In this research work an effort has been made to define music therapy with many references. How music therapy heals is a major concern for the same.

After an effort to understand the definitions of Music therapy, now, under this research work comes, 'The contribution of Indian Music to Music Therapy'. And under this heading it is important to study the power of sound because that's the base of Music. There are many references given in this research work about the Self realization which is the 'Goal of Hinduism'. When we talk of Indian music then it is vital to discuss the role of different forms of Indian Music in healing process and to analyze them from the same point of view. I have come to know about the healing role of Ragas on an important level. The Power of "AUM" which is the Vibration defining the entire COSMOS is immense. It is not only believed by Indians but also on a global level. References are given for the same.

The cultural effect of good music, even if it is wordless, can be considerable. It is a verifiable fact that where the arts are not given the importance they deserve, the popular expression of emotions is often quite chaotic.[2]

India, our country, having the rich cultural values of Indian music is known for its culture throughout the world. The contribution of Indian Music to Music therapy has its own fair account. Still, while studying such a broad topic it is required to mention what is going on round the globe related to Music therapy. An honest effort has been made to quote some researchers, music therapists and their works, beliefs & techniques to know the flow better. So that, in future, the students of Indian music can relate their area of interest accordingly to this field. As, present references always become the ground for future buildings of thoughts and beliefs.

The Cultural Uniqueness and Togetherness of Music Therapy is also a zone to be covered for the well-being of humankind because it can be a good mix of Eastern and a Western Voice regarding the role and implementation on Music Therapy. By studying this we can open a new gate to further research on the Global Music Therapy. By doing so, we can actually prove the healing role of Music and authenticate the existence of Indian Music as a healing power.

In modern times when the music education is on university level, music text books have becomea necessity. For the researchers, who are exploring the various theoretical and historical aspects of music, books are the main source of information. This research work can help at least some of the students of music.

It is said that:

> "A musical child guided under proper surroundings and in the right path is sure to grow obedient, intelligent and sympathetic. A musical soul is like pure gold, and its shape depends upon what its owner gives to it."

Since the day I resolute to learn Indian Classical Music, my life altered significantly. It got focus, concentration, determination, aim and zeal to be a frontrunner amongst all the counterparts. I became a known and acknowledged student academically as well as a winner in various activities like sports, declamations, drama, script writing and most of all reigning pin-up in all music competitions. To my great surprise, my confidence in myself boosted, when I topped the school at the secondary level. It was a memorable triumph for me and my family, and the achievements are still on the roll to be in my lap. When I recall those sudden paradigm shifts or changes in my life at that point of instance it will be attributed to the **'HEALING MUSIC'**. I am indebted to music for bestowing novel magnitude and directions to my existence as psychological, physiological, social and mental healer. After having such astonishing, revolutionized transformations in my own life, it was not possible for me to elude this subject. It's a best occasion and time for me to repay my homage and to magnetize those who are still naive of the important therapeutic character of this enormous art.

While doing my research work, I have learnt a lot and have come to a conclusion that, Indian music is an integral part of Music Therapy and has contributed to this therapeutic field to a great extent from ancient times. Indian Music is a vast ocean full of the references about its healing powers. Though currently a lot of work being done based on Indian music in India and abroad, in a modern way, yet the traditional methods are required to authenticate the process by a deep study and understanding of the past techniques.

At last I would like to conclude with: "'it is very important for the students who are being trained in Indian Music to know the essence and emotions involved in it. Because, Indian music does not only start with seven notes and never ends on a single raga. It has a lot to do with human life and the cultural front of the society. It is said that "A healthy mind stays in a healthy body". On the basis of different references given in this particular research work, we can come to a conclusion that Indian Music has immense power to keep both Mind and Body intact with good health." The contribution of Indian Music to Music Therapy is a very broad topic to cover but I have tried my hardest to do justice to this deep topic to the best of my ability.

CPSIA information can be obtained
at www.ICGtesting.com
Printed in the USA
LVHW040906060423
743581LV00010B/245

9 781805 252795